I0126781

CONVERSING WITH

JAMES HILLMAN

City & Soul

Conversing with

James Hillman

City & Soul

3rd Annual

The Dallas Institute of Humanities & Culture

James Hillman
2014 Symposium

Joanne H. Stroud Series Editor

Robert Sardello Editor

CONVERSING WITH JAMES HILLMAN
City & Soul: James Hillman Symposium 2014
3rd Annual James Hillman 2014 Symposium—*City & Soul* was held October 16-18
The Dallas Institute of Humanities and Culture.

Printed in the United States.

Library of Congress
Stroud, Joanne H.
Conversing With James Hillman City & Soul / introduced by Joanne H. Stroud / edited by Robert Sardello

10 digit–ISBN 0-911005-56-0   13 digit–ISBN 978-0-911005-56-1
Archetype (Psychology)

Grateful acknowledgment is made for permission to reproduce material from the following:
"Ideas I See in Her Art" by James Hillman, reprinted from *Margot McLean.* Copyright ©2002 by Moretti
and Vitali. Reprinted with permission of the publisher.

Margot McLean, *Muscles of Inspiration,* 1989, mixed media on board, 10" x 8" and *Obicularis Oris* (detail),
1990, mixed media on board, 12" x 16". Courtesy of the artist.

"In Memory of Sigmund Freud." Copyright ©1940 and renewed 1968 by W. H. Auden; from *W. H. Auden:
Collected Poems* by W. H. Auden. Used by permission of Random House, an imprint and division of Penguin
Random House LLC. All rights reserved. "The Night, the Porch" from *Blizzard of One: Poems* by Mark
Strand. Copyright ©1998 by Mark Strand. Used by permission of Alfred A. Knopf, an imprint of Knopf
Doubleday Publishing Group, a division of Penguin Random House LLC. All rights reserved. Any third party
use of the above material, outside of publication, is prohibited. Interested parties must apply directly to
Penguin Random House LLC for permission.

Philip Guston, *San Clemente,* 1975. Oil on canvas. 68 x 73 1/4 inches.
Courtesy of The McKee Gallery, New York, New York.

Publications Editors Sarah Theobald-Hall and Laura Gloege
Book design by O! Suzanna, Suzanna L. Brown

The Dallas Institute of Humanities and Culture Publications publishes books that bring
disciplines of the imagination—depth psychology, literary criticism, art, architecture, cultural
criticism—to focus on the revitalization of culture.

The Dallas Institute of Humanities and Culture
2719 Routh Street, Dallas, Texas 75201 USA 214 871-2440

www.dallasinstitute.org

Table of Contents

PART III: Politics of Beauty

PART IV: Places of Practice

PART V: Responsive Environmentalism—The Soul of the City in Distress

More Conversations

Two papers were not presented at the 2014 symposium; they are added here to our explorations.

References

Index

About James Hillman

JAMES HILLMAN (b. 1926 – d. 2011) was a pioneering psychologist whose imaginative psychology has entered cultural history, affecting lives and minds in a wide range of fields. He is considered the originator of Archetypal Psychology. Hillman received his Ph.D. from the University of Zurich in 1959 where he studied with Carl Jung and held the first directorship at the C. G. Jung Institute until 1969. In 1970, he became the editor of **SPRING JOURNAL**, a publication dedicated to psychology, philosophy, mythology, arts, humanities, and cultural issues and to the advancement of Archetypal Psychology. Hillman returned to the United States to take the job of Dean of Graduate Studies at the University of Dallas after the first International Archetypal Conference was held there. Hillman, in 1978 along with Gail Thomas, Joanne Stroud, Robert Sardello, Louise Cowan, and Donald Cowan, co-founded The Dallas Institute of Humanities and Culture in Dallas, Texas. *The Uniform Edition of The Writings of James Hillman* is published by Spring Publications, Inc. in conjunction with The Dallas Institute of Humanities and Culture.

The body of his work comprises scholarly studies in several fields including psychology, philosophy, mythology, art, and cultural studies. For the creativity of his thinking, the author of *A Terrible Love of War* (2004), *The Force of Character and the Lasting Life* (1999), and *Soul's Code: In Search of Character and Calling* (1996) was on the *New York Times* best-seller list for nearly a year. *Re-Visioning Psychology* (1975), which was nominated for a Pulitzer Prize, *The Myth of Analysis* (1972), and *Suicide and the Soul* (1964) received many honors, including the Medal of the Presidency of the Italian Republic. He held distinguished lectureships at the Universities of Yale, Princeton, Chicago, and Syracuse, and his books have been translated into some twenty languages.

The influences shaping the core of Hillman's work are not limited to depth psychology. His ideas have firm grounding in the classical Greek tradition and are also deeply influenced by Renaissance thought and Romanticism, encompassing the contributions of psychologists, philosophers, poets, and alchemists. Hillman described his own line of thought as part of the lineage of Heraclitus, Plato, Plotinus, Vico, Ficino, Schelling, Coleridge, Dilthey, Freud, and Jung. Other influential authors in Hillman´s work are Keats, Bachelard, Corbin, Nietzsche, Paracelsus, and Shelley.

Throughout his writings, Hillman criticized the literal, materialistic, and reductive perspectives that often dominate the psychological and cultural arenas. He insisted on giving psyche its rightful place in psychology and culture, fundamentally through imagination, metaphor, art, and myth. That act he called soul-making, a term borrowed from Keats.

He is recognized as one of the most important radical critics and innovators of contemporary culture.

ROBERT SARDELLO

Preface

A SMALL PHOTOGRAPH of an aged James Hillman hangs on the wall of my study. He walks, his back toward the viewer, down a country road, cane in hand, trees embracing him from each side. The road continues far in front of him. He seems to be in deep thought while engaging in determined movement. He wears a blue cap and a grey sweater with an almost mandala-like pattern, his right leg moving toward the next step, white pant leg ruffled, as if he is running in the wind. How in the world could he be walking with a cane, pant leg furling like that? This is no stroll. The road goes on endlessly, like an image of movement itself. While he seems to be leaving, he also beckons us to walk with him in this manner: reverential toward earth, absorbed in the depths of active thought, determined, receptive, with wisdom-filled seeing that seeking is in the movement itself, with no thought of an ending.

As I hold within and think of James from the heart, I am also transported in reverie to the yearly gatherings at the Dallas Institute of Humanities and Culture, contemplative conferences that are like walking with him on this road. The reveries surprise because inwardly I see each person gathered at these intimate and dynamic conferences smiling, and, as they smile, they are the smile, and the smile is James.

This volume invites you on this walk, with this smile. It is the first of what will be a series of small volumes of ongoing conversations with James on the road. We walk with him now in the manner he so loved, the manner of receiving broad, deep, high, active, and moving thinking, embraced by beautiful language.

The James Hillman Symposiums are more than an inspired idea. They had to happen; how could they not happen? James Hillman and Pat Berry (Hillman) came from Zurich to live in Dallas. So it seems. But for James, living and being and doing were all one, and being in Dallas for him was Being in Dallas, something far different than existing here as a resident. For James, who you are, what you do, and where you are was always one. It is possible, no, it is easy to feel him participating in the conversations at the Dallas Institute, and it is as if these yearly conferences gather what lives silently within the atmosphere of this place.

What perhaps most attracted James to Dallas was an inner vision that the completeness of his work was to be found in bringing into language the presence of the Soul of the World, intimately, insightfully, and practically. He found the seeds of this completeness already happening in Dallas with a small, united group of people who were looking for him before they even knew him.

The participants in these yearly gatherings all seem to be on this road with James. The road is wide, encompassing, and inviting. The conferences follow the brilliant inspiration of Joanne H. Stroud, who announced to us one day that we should form a series of conferences, each concentrating on the theme of one volume of the *Uniform Edition of the Writings of James Hillman*. The conferences were not to interpret the volumes, re-present them in some fashion, critique them, nor analyze them, but rather to walk in conversations with Jim, enter now what is down the road.

This first publication of the series, then, most appropriately intensifies the work of James Hillman concerned with the "Soul of the World," brought together in the second volume of the *Uniform Edition*, entitled *City & Soul*. The range, variety, colors, and tonalities of the papers presented astound—from urban renewal imaginally considered to education as the disruption of commerce to poetic awareness, the subversion, greed, and grief in the city, the body politic, the south of the soul, capitalism and the city, the Soul of Dallas, and so, so much more.

You will find engaging with these papers does something, for they will surprise, turn habitual notions inside out, upside down, and together make something like a Mobius strip within which you know and don't know where you are. Because of this quality of confusion with clarity, we find ourselves changed by immersion in these papers. The writings are inherently therapeutic; they take the patient out of the consulting room and see that now, in our time, the patient is the world. But, good heavens, nowhere will you find a fix suggested!

Healing occurs through entering with awareness what is otherwise felt only as pain and confusion, or mania, or shortsightedness, or one-sidedness, or opportunity for gain. Through awareness, by way of the whole of our Being, we are able to bear the suffering soul of the city in a restorative way. Awareness, though, does not only occur within the awakened individual. Buildings can reveal awareness, and so can politics or economy, or education—that is, the things themselves bear awareness, but only when we are soul-aware. These papers reveal something of this kind of awareness, as well as something else.

The something else . . . these papers stand wonderfully on their own and reveal aspects of the great contribution of archetypal psychology as a method rather than only content. How do they do this? Through language, the great and mighty mystery of language.

Once we become attuned to soul, soul everywhere, language itself perhaps becomes the revealed secret of what counts as archetypal, the revelation of something within and yet beyond what one says or writes. An archetypal nature of language characterizes the change-agent within each of these papers. If we hear or read only the content, then we read something certainly different, content we may not be used to. But inherent within these papers percolates something that we can never become used to. The papers, we might say, are written in archetypally aware language.

Language exists before we begin to speak or write. Without it we could not speak. It is only through the very language of these papers that we begin to feel what is meant by "Soul of the World" and "City and Soul." It is not by the content alone. The informational content of these papers may be counted as minimal. The archetypally aware language proceeds as if a gift is being given, a gift beyond experience and outside us, yet that exists for us. I do not think that any of the presenters in these conferences hold themselves as the sole creators of what they speak. Language can be felt as an archetypal reality.

Language when felt and experienced as a numinous presence raises us up beyond the merely human level. Language, the kind of language by which these papers are written, hovers over and through us like a bright, distant cloud, and the actual writing a yearning that answers and responds to this hovering, beckoning cloud.

The language of these papers comes from a sphere beyond the world of information and utility and thus imbues them with depth. Every one of these papers creates something that is beyond the capacity of the writers, though it is as if the very Being of language lent itself to them to speak in these ways. There are aspects within each of these papers that make the inaudible audible. Mere content, ideas, information, or utility can never do anything of this sort.

The language of these papers dreams itself into the future. These are not papers of fact, or history, or metaphysics, or even psychology; they are more like sculptural gestures that point toward and include us with the actually present ineffable.

This kind of language makes human love possible. I don't think it is possible to read these papers in a truly receptive way without returning to the world, to the city, where we live and work, now noticing the radiance of love within our surrounds. Content alone is incapable of producing this kind of observed and noticed transformation.

These papers are also not merely the papers of individuals, of individual minds. Archetypally inspired language does not exist in such an isolated fashion. Getting together like this, conversationally, under the continuing inspiration of James Hillman, we give one another more than the individual participants intend to give. Language of this sort creates something beyond the capacity of those who use it. The conferences are an offering, an offering through which the seeds of a changed world are being planted, a world in which we can begin again together.

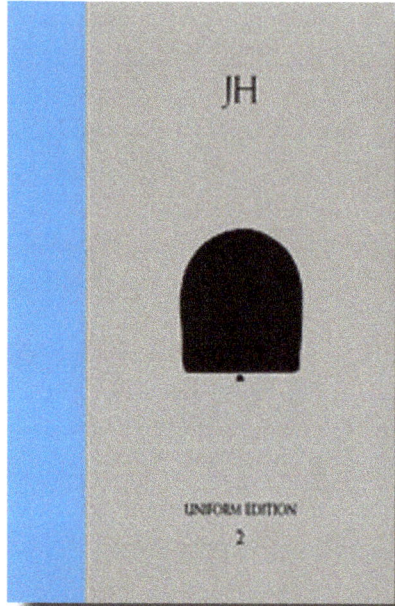

CITY & SOUL
Uniform Edition Vol. 2   JAMES HILLMAN
Edited by Robert J. Leaver   Introduction by Gail Thomas

Forty-two chapters comprise Hillman's writings on the psychology of public affairs: urbanism, environmental aesthetics, citizenship, and politics. The essays and talks divide into four groups: Patient as Citizen; Politics of Beauty; Places of Practice; Responsive Environmentalism.

Spring Publications, in conjunction with The Dallas Institute of Humanities and Culture, publishes the *Uniform Edition of the Writings of JAMES HILLMAN*, the founder of ARCHETYPAL PSYCHOLOGY—the lasting legacy of an original mind.

The Uniform Edition, a clothbound set of 10 volumes of the writings of James Hillman (also available as ebooks), unites major lectures, occasional writings, scholarly essays, clinical papers, and interviews arranged thematically. Each volume is embossed with a drawing by the American artist James Lee Byars.

Introduction

WE MIGHT BEGIN by asking why did James Hillman talk and write enough about the city to fill an entire volume, *City & Soul,* of his *Uniform Edition*? We could speculate that this subject became of major interest to him because in America in the late twentieth century we had grown careless and had allowed so many of our major metropolises to fall into decline. One of the most singular, unique contributions to Western civilization that the city-state of Athens made in the classic era was appreciation for the cohesion of the city. Athenians revered the ideal image of the City, *the Polis*. We still embody the Greek language in the word above, "metropolis." The concentration of populations in city centers brought about liberating ideas of freedom, freedom from the constant struggle merely for survival. By the pooling of work and the division of labor into specialties, the City allowed some leisure time and therefore greater opportunities for the development of culture.

In America in the '80s and '90s, we forgot about these advantages of urban life as masses migrated to the suburbs, leaving cities to fall into dilapidation. This spreading fate of disbursement was certainly true for the center of the city in Dallas, where the "centre could not hold," to borrow from the poet W. B. Yeats on the disintegration of culture. We forgot about the advantages of city life, and ours became a swelling group of office workers in glass high-rise buildings from whose garages working masses claimed their cars and drove away quickly at sundown, leaving the downtown at night—spooky.

With this exodus, "politics," another word derived from the word *polis*, and all things political or civic were abandoned, or left largely to professional politicians. One of the duties of citizenship in the city, to be involved in grassroot politics, was abdicated to others and has never since returned as a central activity or required responsibility of gathering together to further the good of the whole. We could speculate that the ramifications of this move away from civic obligation may be reverberating today in the disarray of political life at the national level.

The Dallas Institute of Humanities and Culture, the site and sponsor of the James Hillman Symposiums, is known for its work of drawing attention to the soul of the City. We never lost our faith in the attraction of a fully functioning city. With our "Center for the City" program and our annual conferences: "What Makes a City?" or "What Does the City Want to Be?" directed by Dr. Gail Thomas, we kept reimagining what a city, a lively one, could be. We reminded ourselves that it was indeed possible to bring back the bustling energy that had fled the center, turning the central area into decrepitude and the suburbs into urban sprawl, for the extended periphery.

In the twenty-first century, the problem of honoring the city and its citizens persists but in an altogether different manner. Inhabitants now are often conceived as consumers rather than as citizens. According to Edwin Heathcote (2015), the English architecture critic, "We have all become data." We are more regarded as numbers to be tracked or targeted than as citizens to contribute to the mix. Also one of the advantages of city life—the combination of anonymity and sociability—the potential of getting lost in a crowd but also of finding friends within walking distance—is disappearing thanks to smartphones and social media. Dallas only recently experienced a turn-around, a revitalization stimulated by the returning of its inhabitants into the center. Dallas is now booming with an air of excitement. However, we do need to avoid gentrification and pay heed to Heathcote's warning: "When cities become too successful, they marginalize exactly the eccentricity and experimentation that lead to new ideas. An overdose of success can kill a city."

The first thing on the agenda at the 2014 symposium was a bus ride to the places of soul in the city of Dallas. Every citizen in every city across the country would gain perspective by taking a tour of his or her town every five years or so. Just asking this question: "What are the places of soul in the city?" and stopping to reflect is an enlightening process. It is not a surprise to us who have long been involved in the reclaiming the city of Dallas to know that each city does indeed have a special soul, and if one but searches, one can feel the connection.

The word "soul" has a complex array of meanings. We are using it here not in the religious sense, though it does connect to that which is eternal, but rather as the essence of what is precious, what arouses butterflies for its beauty or wrenches our hearts by invoking a sense of shared humanity and communality. For simplicity's sake, we could say that Spirit is different from Soul. Matters of Spirit hold sway in the mind, while Soul matters grip our hearts. Gaston Bachelard, the twentieth-century French philosopher of science, beloved by and often quoted in Hillman's works, distinguishes soul from mind in *The Poetics of Space* (1994): "A consciousness associated with the soul is more relaxed, less intentionalized than a consciousness associated with the phenomena of the mind" (p. xxi). Bachelard often uses poetry and poetic images for detailing his point of references, as he does here in defining soul: "The word 'soul' is an immortal word. In certain poems it cannot be effaced, for it is born of our breath" (p. xx). It renders an "Ah, ha, that's it!" of recognition. I always consult Robert Sardello or Thomas Moore when searching for definitions of soul experiences.

Thus, we boarded a bus for a full-day tour in search of some of the most soulful spots in our city. I was amazed at the places that I had not visited, such as the Continental Pedestrian Bridge with its playful attractions connecting in a new, neighborly way Oak Cliff to Dallas along with a spectacular view of the gorgeous Margaret Hunt Hill Bridge designed by Santiago Calatrava, or the grassy knoll with a plaque inscribed with the last words from John F. Kennedy's speech that he would have given here in 1963. Our communal history and memories relate more personally after such a visit. You will read about this experience in Gail Thomas's essay. We returned to the Dallas Institute for an informal outdoor dinner provided by food trucks parked in the driveway between our main building and the Stroud House (yes, there is an imposing, recently purchased, three-story red brick building of which I am exceedingly proud. Several of our presenters inaugurated the Stroud House by staying there).

Indoors Larry Allums, the Executive Director of the Dallas Institute, and I welcomed additional invited guests before Larry read Dr. Louise Cowan's "Remembering James Hillman." We started the evening appropriately by seeing and hearing the recorded voice of James himself in viewing Margot McLean Hillman's excerpts drawn the BBC series *Architecture of the Imagination* in 1993/1994. We are particularly pleased to reprint in this volume an essay "The Ideas I See in Her Art" that Hillman wrote for the book on Margot's paintings published by Moretti and Vitali in 2002, which, if you haven't come across it, may be your only opportunity to read it as it won't be included in future **Uniform Edition** volumes.

I acknowledge the audacity that I feel in tackling the task of properly introducing you to each of our presenters. But here goes, with my apologies if I don't capture the gist of these very rich papers.

The first panel moderated by Robert Sardello set the stage with images of city life, some surprising. Robert Leaver talked about the many similar issues that Dallas shares with the city of Providence, Rhode Island. Robert had the good fortune of working closely with Hillman in editing and formulating this volume, *City & Soul*, and gave us some personal insights. He also wrote the Introduction. Robert Romanyshyn used the image of the bench to illustrate connection in his presentation "Sitting on a Park Bench with James Hillman: Conversations with the Dead." He began by provocatively quoting W. S. Auden: "[T]o us he is no more a person / now but a whole climate of opinion." Nor Hall's witty movement film "What the Foot Wants: City as Set for Movement Theater," shot in the city of Minneapolis, with vivid images of a loose foot in an animated city challenging us to think seriously about how we effect the city, even its traumas, and how in turn it affects us.

Saturday morning we began in earnest to address the sections of the volume *City & Soul,* which is divided into four parts: Patient as Citizen, Politics of Beauty, Places of Practice, and Responsive Environmentalism, respectively. It was a tough assignment to try to do justice to the book in one day of discussion.

I enjoyed serving as the moderator of the first session, Patient as Citizen, with Gustavo Beck Urriolagoitia speaking about "Returning the Soul's Body Politic: Reflections Toward an Imaginal Democracy." He convincingly united his two subjects, politics and psychology, by speaking psychologically about politics

3

and politically about psychology. Randy Severson's "The Dailiest Day" reflected on the city and its effect on Hillman's late life work. He struck a chord with his radical idea of the notion of the soul, the self, as *interiorization of the community*. Mary Watson explained that she and Hillman had discussed the idea of a conference on late-stage capitalism, which Hillman derided as "euphemistically called a 'free market economy,'" holding that it "aims in one direction only. It is single-mindedly obsessed with growth of profit, which throws the shadow of depression into society as downsizing, pink slips, expansion of debt and bankruptcies."

Gail Thomas moderated the next session, Politics of Beauty. In his double role as Curator-at-Large of the Phillips Collection in Washington, D.C., and also Publisher and Editor-in-Chief of Spring Publications, Klaus Ottmann was well qualified to speak about "No Ethics Wthout Aesthetics." He brought up the distinction between an "aesthetic response" and an "ethical response." Sarah Jackson's "When Beauty Walks a Razor's Edge—How our Sense of Beauty Grows and Changes" seemed to answer perfectly Hillman's request that psychology "reinvent itself as an aesthetic activity." By sticking with the image, in her example of a painting at first considered weird or ugly and allowing it to have its effect on the viewer, we can be surprised to discover its beauty. Dennis Slattery in "The Aesthetics of the City: Moments of Arrest" engaged Hillman's argument against separating out beauty as a quality only of proportion or of nature, instead insisting that the daily order of mundane things also can embody beauty. Matthew Green's "Teaching Poetic Awareness" detailed how exchange students become more aware of the textures, tastes, smells, and colors of their environment after experiencing a semester of sensory engagement with a foreign city (in this case Toulouse, France). This expanding of consciousness opens a pathway toward overcoming the "psychic numbing" (Robert Lifton's term) that is so prevalent due to the overdose of information.

Scott Churchill moderated the third session, Places of Practice. Rodney Teague in "Going to Town, Being in Town, Leaving Town" took issue with Hillman's favoring the city cousin (or mouse) over the country cousin, while finally acknowledging that Hillman's central theme is that one does not have to go out into nature to find rewarding experiences. The city also provides these. Cheryl Sanders-Sardello in "You Have the Right to Remain Silent" argued for the fecundity of silence. She drew many examples of its complexity and its comfort. She amplified Hillman's view of how a depth of silence permeates even the loudest of cities, functioning as the holder of the true potential of soul-making and allowing us to see closely, through the heart. Gustavo Barcellos in his "South and the Soul" reminded us that Hillman spoke many times of the appeal of moving the entire study of psychology "southward." As a native of Brazil, he was singularly qualified to speak of what it means to be from the south, a South American. He addressed perceptions that produce dark projections not only of anything south of the Equator but also of going downward or "south" to find soul.

Larry Allums moderated the fourth, final session of a long, rewarding day. I had the pleasure of speaking first, happy to lead so that I could actively listen to the two other presenters in our panel. My presentation made the case for "responsive environmentalism," the awareness that one finds over and over in Hillman's works of honoring the fabric of life that surrounds us, whether deemed efficient or not. Scott Becker used two provocative images in his "The Minotaur and the Matrix: Technology and the Soulless City" to delve into the way technology has altered relationships in the city. He spoke of the longing for silence with the incessant buzz of digital devices and the longing for connectedness in the soulless city. Robert Sardello concentrated in his "Between Greed and Grief: The Imaginal Space of the City" on the un-acknowledged grief that accompanies greed principally in our larger cities. As an example he traced the historical founding of New York City. As usual Sardello kept his listeners (and readers, too) focused on avoiding the all-too-simple, the smug or the hyped view of economic life while providing a fulsome psychological understanding of some of the invisible depths of city life in America.

Two papers were not presented at the 2014 symposium, those of Tom Cheetham, "Urban Renewal," and Jonathan Harrell, "Longing for Ugliness," but they added to our explorations and are included in this volume.

Remembering Hillman's special way of synthesizing and bringing together in unique patterns the entire body of Judeo-Christian thought and experience with his special witty touch reminded the group that we are indeed soul mates in this endeavor. This is especially true of Gail Thomas, Robert Sardello, and me, all three of us Founding Fellows of the Institute, along with Louise Cowan and of the two who are no longer with us, Donald Cowan and, of course, James Hillman. We have long and happily shared in the care of the Dallas Institute, the care of the city, and the care for soul matters. Larry Allums and Claudia Allums, Director of the Cowan Teachers Institute, as well as Cheryl Sanders-Sardello have joined us, and I want to thank each of them for their ongoing and supportive friendship. Emily Hargrove, then Director of Development and Communication, and now Director at the Dallas Festival of Ideas, made a major contribution to the success of the 2014 symposium by arranging for a most delicious lunch under crystal chandeliers at the historic downtown Neiman Marcus and also by following every activity with her camera. Suzanna Brown brings her acute awareness of aesthetics to every endeavor of book design. We work together happily on all publications, including the program. I could not get along without Kim McBride and Sarah Theobald-Hall in their caring attention to the many details of the symposium, making certain that all our visitors felt the hospitality of our city. They also played a major part in this book. The staff of the Institute, including Jonathan Harrell, Jordan Cooper, and Joshua Kalin, added their individual touches to make the three days spent together memorable.

As a coda, as a vignette, and as an example of attentive responsiveness, I would like to cite Thomas Moore's book, *Soul Mates: Honoring the Mysteries of Love and Relationship*. This little paragraph is testimony to the power of soul connection:

> After all, what the soul wants is attachment—a detached friend-ship is a contradiction in terms. Therefore, like all forms of soulful living, friendship demands attention. We may be present to our friend through visits, phone calls, letters, or postcards. Using any method at hand, we can nurture a friendship through simple heart-felt expressions. Some of my most treasured tokens of friendship are postcards with only a half-sentence on them, best if the half-sentence is thoughtful, or if it conjures up some intimacy between me and the sender. I have treasured a postcard from James Hill-man that reads simply, "My health? Root canal and spreading bad poison ivy, and yours? (p. 95)

All in all, engaging and conversing with Hillman's *City & Soul* was illuminating, and I and many others present felt that we needed to continue our discussions, so rich was this collection of essays. Not only does James Hillman have much to add to knowledge of the experience of life in the city, but he also leaves us with much to further question. My hope is that this new book, *Conversing with James Hillman*, will provide that opportunity for its readers.

Muscles of Inspiration, 1989, mixed media on board, 10" X 8" Copyright © Margot McLean

JAMES HILLMAN

Ideas I See in Her Art

THE WORLD PRESENTS a layout of surfaces. Surfaces afford information and express intentions in their display as images. Whatever subjectivity there might be immanent in the world, whatever its potentials of consciousness—innate intelligibility, symbolic significance, desire to be appreciated, and appeal to be loved and feared—are manifested in surfaces and displayed as images.

A Layout of Surfaces – This fundamental idea by which I perceive McLean's paintings has been elaborated by J.J. Gibson and his psychological school of "direct perception." An animal lives in a world of directly perceivable information-laden images. Its instinct is attuned with surfaces and it does not only resort to learning and memory for its immediate being in the world. A similar idea permeates the great work of the Swiss zoologist Adolf Portmann (whose work is familiar to McLean): the inwardness of living forms is exhibited in surface display. Close and comparable are the phenomenological examinations into the perceptual world by Merleau-Ponty, and Gaston Bachelard's inquiry into elemental images as primary to human awareness.

In short: "The depths are on the surface" (Wittgenstein). McLean's work asserts the primacy of surfaces. They are its content. They are treated to give palpable texture and layered differentiation in order to accrete intensity to surface as dominant fact of the image, any image. Her images are intensities of surfaces. The illusory content of her paintings—tree, flower, animal—are seductive foci, not subjects, of the image. The subject is the subjective intensity of the image as such.

Since even a surrealist perspective that reaches out into immensities of distance is only a millimeter thick, paintings mimic the world as a layout of surfaces. This mimesis does not copy the world as literal naturalists attempt, but rather shares with the world the same phenomenological, even ontological, foundation: showing forth inwardness in the surface of the images. The world too is a *trompe l'oeil.*

Images Must Be Imagined – "Between the concept and the image, there is no synthesis"; "the image can only be studied through the image" (Bachelard). Neither perception, nor the idea, nor symbol, nor natural fact is the source (foyer) or home of the image. Only in imagination are images at home. This "imagination," however, has its own domain, which is only partly in the chambers of the brain. [The brain reforms the imaginal into idiosyncratic expression compatible with

15

the brain's individualized complexity; but the brain does not originate the eternality of the imaginal, its archetypal significances, its "esemplastic" (Coleridge) power.]

Concepts applied to images serve only to coalesce their polysemous presence into sweeping categories, reductive labels, and/or mission statements from the artist, the critic, or the "school." Words do not merely fail; they simply do not apply. Where do we "put" McLean's paintings? Are they modernist or post-modern? Abstract or figurative? Environmental landscapes or psychological inscapes?

The divisions dominating art-talk such as the classical genres (portrait, landscape, narrative, still-life) or more contemporary ones (abstract, figurative, conceptual, environmental, minimalist, etc.) reveal less about the painted image than about the inadequacy of concepts for placing, especially if the "place" of the painting is imagination as well as nature. [Constable, we may remember, said: "The whole object and difficulty of the art (indeed of all the fine arts) is to unite imagination with nature"]. Can we not surpass the hackneyed terms by following the paintings themselves into another terrain where nature's imagination shows as an imagined nature which calls for other principles altogether, old ones, such as vision, soul, beauty?

Epistrophé (or Restoration) – Art intends to restore the fallen world. It has a program—a program, however, that does not stem from the will of the artist but emerges from the image as the image develops in the artist's service to it. If, as Neoplatonism in its many varieties claims, all things desire to return to their sources (*epistrophé*), the temporal to the eternal (and the eternal is not the perfect but itself distorted with the sublime peculiarities of the Gods, as myths tell us), so each artwork attempts to reach beyond itself in implicative power. It attempts to implicate the further in the nearer, the pleroma in the plain, the cosmos in a grain of sand. This power that the artwork attempts to implicate by its very artfulness is called, in human languages, beauty. As the image moves toward beauty, allowing more and more beauty to appear in the world, the world is reminded of its origins and what it longs for. Art evokes longing; it must be nostalgic, and because its ultimate standard is the ultimate itself, beyond possibility, each art work is always incomplete.

The measure of success of a painting lies in its *epistrophé*, which I suggest is the most embracing and accurate conceptual category by which art may be judged and under which other categories (technique, style, formal arrangement, mastery of materials, intellectual cohesion, spontaneity, etc.) must be subsumed. These dissections do not carry the work to its source; they break it down into its components. They tell something of how it is "put together" but not of its power to transport beyond itself, the image that desires its return, belaboring the artist with incessant impulsions and critiques. It directs the work toward its aim, which is what Plato called the beautiful.

Mapping – It thus becomes evident why McLean turned to maps to settle the location of her oeuvre. Body parts, animal species, place names—the titles given to earlier paintings attempted to place the images "somewhere." The map, however, attempts to depict the somewhere as such. The place of a McLean map is a non-place, utopic in the sense of Henry Corbin's philosophy of the imaginal.

If landscapes present the world's body as a layout of surfaces, the maps carry the landscape into the invisible body that is not anywhere (utopic) and carry the painting itself into a mythic geography such as Borges writes of, and the mystics of Corbin's Sufism describe in detailed splendor.

Such maps are not maps of or symbolic of. Rather they symbolize with (to use Corbin's term) a world that is the imaginal, that is, they are like a poetic account ("*reçit*" in Corbin's language) of visionary accuracy. Such mappings are not lesser derivatives, symbols pointing to the invisible, but are a confluence of another place and the framed place of the painting. Both together. *Con*-fluent, *sym*-bolic both mean "with." So the locus of the mapped is neither here nor there. It sets forth a colored and ordered ever-available hinterland or imaginal terrain, affording the imagination the specific environmental contours of its home territory. As images, these maps are the territory.

Color – The reach of heaven into the world after the catastrophic flood in the Bible shines forth in the rainbow. Its multicolored display heals the breach that ruptured between divine and earthly. When the rainbow appears, heaven and earth touch visibly, sensually. Color is the connection. The rainbow lays out a transparent surface; it is all surface, its body consisting of color.

A spiritual bias assumes that the nowhere and invisible must be abstracted of all sensual elements, purified of colors. This privative understanding of "*no*"-where deprives the geography of the imaginal, and the imagination itself, of its rich variety, reducing it to a colorless metaphysical abstraction—all light, or white, or absolutely black.

McLean's palette derives from both ends of the rainbow: both the evaporating transparent at one end and the gritty loam of actual earths at the other. Both utopic and the topoi (places) of mundane representation. The paintings do not avoid representation by ironic distortions or anti-natural coloring. In fact, color may quite deliberately follow nature—white ducks, brown soil, green leaves—without conceding that color is either representational, symbolic, or personally expressive. The hues in a painting refer to one another in the image. Their selection and juxtaposition are determined by the painting, only secondarily by the items and areas painted.

If heaven shines in the rainbow and the rainbow heals the breach, then colors are means of recall. To be colored is to be touched by the rainbow, restoring the fallen world from its only-earthbound necessities.

The Painted Image – The painted image consists mainly of paint, of course. So literalists of this truth paint paint. Let the paint do the work—color-field, stripes, drippings, tracks of squirts actively entangled. But paint does not become image unless it imagines beyond its necessity (there must be paint to paint) to imply a domain where images have their home, which the image symbolizes with, does not refer to but defers to.

The imaginal is in the paint itself as color, but not simply in the tube or pot of pigment. Although it is there by virtue of the rainbow, the color must be laid out, become a surface by the hand work, hard work, of painting.

Artists of paint are called painters because their actions charge paint with implication by means of surfacing it. Nothing better exemplifies the motto "the depths are on the surface" than the act of laying out the deep pot or thick blob of paint thinly onto the surface; painting as surfacing, paint into image.

Still, not all people who paint are painters, only those who succeed in painting an image. What, then, makes an image besides the necessary surfacing of paint? The wish of the painter? The representation achieved? Not even the devotion of the painter can assure success; nor can the skill, mastery, emotional intelligence, or original invention. The successful image is measured from the non-human other side: by how near the painted image arrives at its impossible goal, the image imagined, the image at home in the invisible non-place of the imaginal.

How arrive there? Certainly not by faithful verisimilitude of the fallen world, nor by its brilliant distortion; but rather by magically enhancing the earthly common (I think of the Dutch, e.g., Vermeer and Van Gogh), or also carrying back or breaking through the evident to the invisible, the "merely" imagined. Only by opening the here to what is not here gains entrance, because it acknowledges that the values by which success is judged are themselves not altogether mundane.

Long ago, in recognition of the transmundane allusion of the image, images were often gilded, bejeweled, so as to approximate what was imagined to be the beauty of the imaginal. Now other techniques attempt this approximation to the utopic: debriding, rubbing out, texturing, layering. All these are used by McLean in order to work through the given, reducing its opacity so that something else, somewhere else can shine through. McLean achieves a radiance of surface without resorting to brightness or sheen or to precise elucidation of figure. Depth solidifies on the surface, bringing illumination from behind, beauty epiphanizing in the subtly altered material, appearing where the painting has undergone a process destructive of its physical substance.

Debriding the image becomes a via negative to beauty, stating in paint that beauty is not quite presented or represented. It is rather as Plotinus indicated, a divine enhancement of earthly things always available—providing the painter prepares a place for it to show.

Insight – Many of McLean's works have little areas set apart like recessed windows and doors. The eye goes further in, drawn less by perspective to a wider farther scene following the paths of nature, but more narrowed and focused following the laws of psychological attention inward toward insight. We are beckoned by these apertures towards an *aperçu*, an insight. We are asked to see through to another layout. As Gibson says, more and more is afforded to perception the more we attend to what is presented.

Seeing through to further potentials within the same image, images within images, places the entire painting within the framework of metaphor. The image works at what it presents and works through it, adding further dimensions by deconstructing what is first only apparently given. These doors of perception insist upon seeing through. They are graphic descriptions of insight.

Arrest – Images arrest. They stop us up, bring us to a standstill. That is their first effect and a prime measure of their success. Interruption, surprise, stopping—the flow of time is invaded by the timeless. Arrest is a consequence of beauty, a way in which beauty shows its power and announces its presence.

Images are like rituals, or, an image is a ritual in brief. Rituals alter time by repetition. They do not move forward and, by repeating movements, they arrest time's progress. We go back and do the act again and come out where we have already been—but not quite. What has been added is not sheer additive repetition—again and again and again. Rather, the bald fact of repetition gives to each repeated occasion, no matter how tiresomely many, the added value of having been worth repeating. It is as if the multiplication of an event confirms its worth (not increases that worth.) Thus does ritual ennoble the most simple mundane action. Thus, too, rituals cannot conclude, climax, or resolve. They are not narratives advancing to a next phase, a further step. No, ritual stops the very idea of progression, because a ritual action goes back into, onto itself, stops with itself, fulfilling itself, self-satisfied. It is this closure of ritual (not its concluding) that aligns ritual with image. For both, the terminal point is arbitrary—when is a painting "finished"? Because ritual and image are saturated and satiated by themselves, they are able to offer satisfaction, completion, fulfillment to their participants.

The framed image, and McLean's are often square as well, stops at its edge, leading nowhere (or only to the utopic *no*-where of its intention). Instead of beginning, middle, and end, instead of the dramatic process of living, there is only repletion of the actual image and the simultaneity of its display. All there at once. Image as slowed epiphany, revealing what it affords only to the eye that deepens its corresponding intensity. So the eye darts, glances, shifts, squints, trying to grasp this concurrent immediacy (of everything at once.)

In this way images break the logical and narrative movement of understanding. The iconic nature of the image is inevitably klastic. The mind, however, broken into by the image, clings to a story about where the image came from, what influenced it, who painted it, and how it belongs within a context: personal history, art history, world history. Defenses against the image; defenses against breakdown.

Nonetheless, the image captivates, again like a ritual. You can't get away from its spell. The viewer struggles; we move close to examine, back off, stand to the side. We seem unable to be as still as the image and find its demand for reciprocal stillness intolerable. We too have been framed, caught, arrested. Then, finally, perception, released from its habits of understanding, begins to see what the image affords.

Obicularis Oris (detail), 1990, mixed media on board, 12" x 16" Copyright © Margot McLean

PART I:

CITY AND SOUL

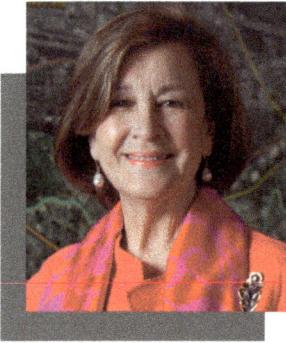

Gail Thomas, Ph.D., serves as President and CEO of The Trinity Trust Foundation in Dallas to remake the Trinity River Corridor. She was co-founder in 1980 of the Dallas Institute of Humanities and Culture and served as its Director for seventeen years. Dr. Thomas' life work has been the study and transformation of cities. For over thirty years she has conducted seminars and conferences on cities and city life. She began in 1982 a series of conferences called *What Makes a City?*, attended by city planners, artists, scientists, poets, teachers, and business and civic leaders. She was instrumental in the creation of Pegasus Plaza in downtown Dallas and co-chaired the Dallas Millennium Project to restore Dallas' icon, Pegasus, the Flying Red Horse. For the Trinity project, her efforts helped inspire the philanthropic gifts for the design of Dallas' two Santiago Calatrava bridges. She is currently seeking funds to build the Trinity Spine Trail from the Audubon Center in southern Dallas to White Rock Lake. Her book *Healing Pandora: The Restoration of Hope and Abundance* was released in 2009. Her other books include: *Stirrings of Culture*, with Robert Sardello; *Images of the Untouched*, with Joanne Stroud; *Imagining Dallas*; and *Pegasus, the Spirit of Cities*. She has a book in progress entitled *Recapturing the Soul of the City*.

GAIL THOMAS
Touring Dallas
with Archetypal Imagination

RECALLING THE DAY James Hillman phoned from Thompson, Connecticut, I remember him asking me to write the Introduction to the second volume of the *Uniform Edition*; "Just a little 'hello' . . . ," he said, "to open the door." In keeping with that tradition, it seems appropriate to offer "just a little 'hello'" for this 2014 gathering of our annual James Hillman Symposium, and we begin with a tour of our city, Dallas.

James Hillman's focus on "city and soul" began in Dallas after he relocated from Zurich in the late 1970s. He resided here, coming in and out, until the mid 1980s. Many of our contributors represented in the following papers have been with us in some capacity during the past thirty-five years. Others, however, have come from various parts of the world and are not familiar with this extraordinarily contradictory place we call Dallas. As Hillman said in his introductory remarks before the Dallas City Council in 1982: "Imagine . . . Dallas!" He always seemed surprised that he had chosen Dallas as his reentry to the United States after so many years as an expatriate. But he did come, joining Robert Sardello, Joanne Stroud, Donald and Louise Cowan, and myself, all engaged in various ways together at the University of Dallas. And he left his mark on us and on our city.

And so we begin our tour.

Dallas soil offers riches for imaginal tilling. Regardless of the depth of excavation, one confronts a conundrum. Known for Big Oil and Big Hair and Neiman Marcus, over 40% of Dallasites live at poverty level; white flight has removed our middle- and upper-class families from public schools (4% Anglo), but paradoxically Dallas boasts the top-ranked U.S. high school—the Talented and Gifted Magnet School in Oak Cliff.

Amazing shifts abound. Remarkable phenomena are appearing, much like the occurrence in nature in the back woods of East Texas when a lake turns over. No one can explain it. Fish and other aquatic creatures die and float to the surface. The smell unbearable—the stench of rotten, decaying carcasses, baking in the hot Texas sun. And then, just as suddenly, the lake seems fresh and new once more. As Gerard Manley Hopkins (1877) said, "nature is never spent. There lives the dearest freshness, deep down things." And so with our city Dallas, having just commemorated the 50th anniversary of the assassination of our 35th President, John Fitzgerald Kennedy. Fifty years after this foul and heinous deed occurred in Dallas, and caused us who lived here at the time to suffer the arrows of hate and blame from throughout the world, we now embrace the influx of hundreds of thousands moving into our region because of our good economy and low cost of living. Go figure.

And James Hillman did. When he arrived in the late '70s, Dallas was suffering from the aftermath of the assassination of the President, and of being branded "the City of Hate." Mayor J. Eric Jonsson had established Goals for Dallas following the 1963 tragedy, and began a ground up, grassroots reimagining of our city. Louise and Donald Cowan were friends of Jonsson and were involved from the beginning. I was invited to join the Urban Design Task Force in the early '70s. Around the same time, Robert Sardello (chair of the Psychology department at the University of Dallas and later Director of the Institute of Philosophic Studies), Joanne Stroud, and I (both doing graduate work there—she was teaching, and I was assistant to the President and later Director of the Center for Civic Leadership) were reading Jung together at informal sessions. One day Sardello brought with him a book by James Hillman. That was it. Within months, Hillman and Patricia Berry were in Dallas, and we were planning the First International Archetypal Psychology Conference, which was held in January 1977. James brought Spring Publications from Zurich to the University of Dallas, and then, after we moved into our house on Routh Street, to the Dallas Institute of Humanities and Culture.

This stirring of culture in Dallas began to show itself in the things of our city. Our "What Makes a City" conferences brought in the wise ones about city and urban life—Jane Jacobs, Holly Whyte, Arthur Erickson, Vincent Scully, Denise Scott-Brown, Roberta Gratz, Ed Bacon, Christian Norberg-Schulz, Weiming Lu, James Rouse, Christopher Alexander, along with poets Kathleen Raine, Wendell Berry, and Dan Kemmis, spiritual visionaries Keith Critchlow and Ivan Illich, and at Hillman's invitation, Adolph Guggenbühl Craig, Wolfgang Geigerich, and Alfred Ziegler. Even after leaving Dallas for Connecticut in the '80s, Hillman always returned to participate in these conferences about the soul of the city.

Much has changed in the thirty years since Hillman addressed City Hall on the soul of the city. The wave of New Urbanism spreads wholesale in city planning, creating humane forces at work, countering twentieth-century goals of efficiency and productivity. One direct result of Hillman's presence in Dallas stems from his attention to the need for beauty in the city. In 2006, the Dean of the School of Architecture in Arlington, Texas came to me saying he had suggested the topic of "Beauty" as the theme for the Texas Society of Architects Conference to be held in Dallas, having been inspired by reading the work of James Hillman. By his own confession, this would be a remarkable moment for the architectural academy. It was a bold move, indeed, initiating a conversation about 'Beauty' in a public forum. The topic had been banished from public discourse for three decades, indeed since before WWI—three-quarters of a century. The subject of beauty, formerly anathema, fueled a flame in the heart of architects and planners.

Today, Dallas' newest landmark—the bridge by Santiago Calatrava—exists because of the reawakened acknowledgment of the soul's hunger for beauty. In May 1998, Dallas passed a bond program to make funds available to enhance the Trinity River corridor. Suddenly, Dallasites were inspired to create something beautiful in our abandoned downtown that would draw people back to the center of the city. We arranged for not one, but two Calatrava bridges to grace our city, and created the motto "Bridging the Trinity for the Love of the City" to bring our citizens together after two centuries of having been divided by the river.

> *I do believe that were the public to awaken to its hunger for beauty there would be rebellion in the streets. Was it not aesthetics that took down the Berlin Wall and opened China? Not market consumerism and Western gadgets, as we are told, but music, color, fashion, shoes, fabrics, films, dance, lyrics, and the shapes of cars.* (Thomas, 2006, Introduction to *City & Soul*, p. 14)

Figure 1.1. Margaret Hunt Hill Bridge, designed by Santiago Calatrava. Copyright ©2015 by Carolyn Brown.

Santiago Calatrava's Bridge

The tour of Dallas began by driving across the elegantly beautiful Margaret Hunt Hill Bridge that spans the Trinity River (fig. 1.1). We stopped on the banks of West Dallas, formerly known during Hillman's time in Dallas as the "back wards" of the city, now newly reinvented as "Trinity Groves," the go-to place for lovers of cosmopolitan food. We walked out on the Continental Bridge (adjacent to Calatrava's bridge), recently converted from a vehicular bridge to one for pedestrians and bikers. This small bridge, opened last June, has already become a central gathering place for families living in the area. Wildly popular, the bridge inspires the local community to host early morning yoga on the bridge and late evening dancing. A meditation labyrinth graces the center portion of the bridge; spray fountains and climbing walls enchant the young ones, while chess and bocce ball entertain an older crowd.

From this vantage point of the "New Dallas," we boarded the bus and braced ourselves for our next stop, Dallas' wound: the Stillpoint.

The Sixth Floor Museum

Few words were spoken here. No words were needed.

We visited the grassy knoll and read the newly laid plaque at the top of the knoll—occasioned on the 50th anniversary of JFK's death, and made available by friend Nancy Cain Marcus (fig. 1.2). The plaque reminds us of the final words in the speech President Kennedy had planned to give at the luncheon in the Dallas Trade Mart: " . . . except the Lord keep the city, the watchman waketh but in vain."

Figure 1.2. Anniversary Marker for Site of John F. Kennedy's Assassination. Copyright ©2015 by Carolyn Brown.

Pegasus Plaza

Our next stop on the tour was Pegasus Plaza (fig. 1.3), where we read the words carved into the granite wall bracing the fountain at the epicenter of the city—the corner of Main and Akard: *"Where the hoof hits the ground, a well springs forth, and the muses come to dance and sing."* We seek a poetic basis of mind. We stick to the image. Pegasus has been the image of Dallas for almost a century (fig. 1.4).

Figure 1.3. Carved Wall at Pegasus Plaza. Copyright ©2015 by Carolyn Brown.

The myth of Pegasus seems to tell the story of Dallas. Christian Norberg Shulz claims every city has its own *genius loci*, which guides and shapes its architecture and even its institutions—the soul of the city, the lay of the land, the way the winds blow, and the waters flow. The myth of Pegasus suggests the story of imagination itself. Images abound in the name—*pegae* in Latin connotes spring; in *equus* we find *agua*, water. Pegasus springs, soaring from impossible odds, the bloody severed head of the Medusa—that which (if literalized) turns one to stone. Out springs Pegasus with golden wings to cure the ills of society. Athena, goddess of the city, has provided Bellerophon the Golden Bridle with which to capture the winged horse and mount him. Together Pegasus and Bellerophon soar about to kill the voracious Chimera. Bellerophon (brother to Pegasus because he also is a son of Poseidon) attempts to ride Pegasus to the heavens. Pegasus, however, as an instrument of the gods, defies his brother's hubristic ambition, throws off the young hero, and soars to the heavens to take his immortal place as a constellation in the heavens. Sticking with the image of the city, the statue of Athena, goddess of the city, shows the birth of Pandora on her base, the Medusa on her breastplate, and winged Pegasus on her helmet.

Figure 1.4. Pegasus Sign, Downtown Dallas. Copyright ©2015 by Carolyn Brown.

Neiman Marcus

As a tribute to Hillman, who loved extravagance, we ended our tour of Dallas with an exclusive lunch, courtesy of Joanne Stroud, served to us in a private dining room on the second floor of Neiman Marcus. The president of Neiman's greeted us and regaled us with stories about the flagship store as marking the very history of Dallas itself. We paused to say goodbye at the entrance of Neiman Marcus on Ervay Street, noticing that the columns at the entrance doors, erected in 1914, are capped with images of Pegasus (fig. 1.5). Indeed, the muses have come to dance and sing.

Figure 1.5. Pegasus on columns at Neiman Marcus Ervay Street entrance, Downtown Dallas.

And so the door is open, after this "little hello," for you to ponder the following essays, as we remember the remarkable contribution of the life work of James Hillman. *"And what is our task? To take this fragile, suffering world up into our arms and transform it"* (Rainer Maria Rilke).

And what is our task?

To take this fragile, suffering world

up into our arms and transform it.

– Rainer Maria Rilke

Robert Leaver is the editor of *City & Soul*, Volume II of the *Uniform Edition of the Writings of James Hillman*. A community psychologist, he has 42 years of experience organizing over 800 community-place -based projects for clients, mostly locally and regionally. As a social entrepreneur, Leaver helped develop many long-standing organizations, including the New England Sustainable Energy Association (NESEA) and the Entrepreneurship Forum of New England (EFNE), a professional guild for entrepreneurs, creators, investors, and resource providers, founded in 2001. He is the founder and convener of New Commons—a think tank founded in 1982 and located in Providence, Rhode Island. It is place-based with that place being a city, an island, a village, an organization, or a wild card—all with soul. New Commons' clients—cities, villages and human networks—need tangible results, so it helps them build a fresh network composed of the right capabilities, and then mobilizes that network of know-how to get the job done: Think, Link, Do. Leaver's project work and writing focus on shaping our culture, locally and regionally. The work is also place-based with the whole mattering more than the parts. This work combines bringing forward the past, especially soul, with what comes next. Handling the tensions of the past and the future is a constant, creative pursuit. Specifically his work and writing are about business and ecology; change and what holds constant; city and soul; digital technology and culture; next economy and place; makers and movers; organizations and whole systems; teaching and learning; resilient and sustainable communities. Leaver is also an Eagle Scout.

ROBERT LEAVER

Creating Volume II of the Uniform Edition of the Writings of James Hillman: City & Soul

I WILL BEGIN with some images of "city and soul" selected by Phil Cousineau (2001) from Hillman's early essay of the same name:

> Without images we tend to lose the way. . . . The soul wants its images, and when it doesn't find them, it makes substitutes: billboards and graffiti, for instance. . . . How do we see into each other, look at each other's faces, read each other—that is how soul contact takes place. . . . We also need body places. Places where bodies see each other, meet each other, are in touch with each other, like the people who leave their offices in Paris and swim in the Seine River. . . . This emphasizes the relationship of the body to the daily life of the city, bringing one's physical body into the city. In other words, I am emphasizing the place of intimacy within a city, for intimacy is crucial to the soul. . . . A city that neglects the soul's welfare makes the soul search for its welfare in a degrading and concrete way, in the shadow of those same gleaming towers . . . the soul that is uncared for turns into an angry child. (qtd. in Cousineau, p. 223)

Engendering city and soul is people noticing and engaging other people as well as the things and conditions of the city, especially each of us sensing and noticing more of the details and particulars—and not generalizing. This move requires us moving slower in the city. City and soul is reflected in the memory layers that are current preoccupations and aspirations. The city is never trapped in past time; instead it unfolds as time changes.

James Hillman taught me to "be a therapist" that shapes places and ideas, and not individual leaders. In effect, focus on how a place shapes us and we shape it. New Commons consults on comprehensive plans for cities and towns, which, historically, are too built-environment centric, paying scant attention to the economy, ecology, or culture of a place. Hillman revealed the vitality of beginning planning with the present and future culture—the soul of a place—then ecology and economy, leaving the built environment for last. This approach reverses the historical planning sequence. This is heresy in professional planning.

Finding the Soul of Providence

I was born in Providence, Rhode Island in 1947, and I will die there—it is my city. In 1948, my parents moved to the suburb of Barrington, fifteen minutes southwest of the city, to be safer and for the kids to go to "better schools." We would visit my aunts, uncles, grandparents, and cousins in the city, but I always sensed that my dad was not at ease driving into or being in the city. Even though he grew up in Providence, the rural and natural feeling of Barrington was more liking to his soul.

Fast forward to 1966, when I enrolled in Roger Williams College in Providence where the campus was spread among many buildings throughout the city. I learned Providence by walking it. In 1967 I joined a seminar by the president of Roger Williams College, on the future of higher education, and he invoked the founding story of Providence by Roger Williams: He was tossed out of Boston with a warrant for his arrest. He was banned from Boston because he spoke against the "shining city upon a hill," the image in which Boston wanted to create itself as "purely" Puritan with no outliers. Instead, he said, Providence would welcome all faiths to "go forth as a bold and lively experiment for the religious or soul freedom for all," a founding statement embedded in the Constitution of Rhode Island. To this day I hold Williams' mantra for Providence as my calling for the work I do in the city and other cities.

Finding Hillman

I first read Hillman in the mid '80s, but not about city and soul. I then met him as a teacher at my second men's retreat in 1989 with Robert Bly and Michael Meade. On the first evening Hillman played catch with me and a bunch of men, which was a treat, because here was a giant thinker, a famous guy, just hanging out. Interestingly, I found my way to city and soul through Gail Thomas and her work in Dallas, and through Robert Sardello's book, *Facing the World with Soul* (1994), especially the chapter, "House and City."

Editing City & Soul

In June 2003, when my son Diego was fourteen months old, my wife, Michelle, and I attended a Hillman weekend workshop in Connecticut. At the close of the Friday talk I approached him to suggest it was time to consider compiling his papers, and I wanted to edit the volume on cities. I had a thin folder of seven or eight pieces, including the 1970s "City & Soul" pamphlet from the Dallas Institute of Humanities and Culture. He paused for a split second, and with those piercing eyes said "no," then walked away. In the morning he called me over and said he had been tired last night and responded in haste. He said the idea of organizing his papers was a good nudge, and he would like me to edit *City & Soul*.

What I thought would be a thin volume based on the size of my skimpy folder of seven or eight pieces turned into 42 pieces and easily could have been bigger because he kept sending me material, and I would scour online as well.

When we started compiling the volume, only one of the 42 pieces was electronically stored—"City, Soul, and Myth"—a talk he did in Providence in 2005 for a conference I helped organize on the Transformation of Cities (more on that shortly). The other 41 pieces were either Xerox copies of an article, a tape to transcribe, a typed talk with his handwritten inserts and cross-outs, or a handwritten talk. Some articles had to be shortened to reduce repetition. Some articles were combined because they had the same text under the same theme in both.

The book was edited the old-fashioned way, without the use of digital technology, until the end when the articles were electronically organized on a disc. It was a slow, deliberate, and sometimes tense three-year unfolding. Thompson, Connecticut (where Hillman lived), and Providence, Rhode Island are 45 minutes apart so we met in person, talked on the phone, sent mail to each other, and exchanged faxes. It took three years, from the idea in June 2003, to complete the editing in June 2006 when it was handed to Klaus Ottmann, the editor of Spring Publications. There was still a lot of work for Klaus to do because many Greek words got lost in translation. Hillman and I disagreed on which article to end with. I wanted "City, Soul, and Myth," and he wanted "Ground Zero: A Reading." It ends with "Ground Zero," as you knew it would, knowing Hillman. In late 2006, volume two of the *Uniform Edition of the Writings of James Hillman, City & Soul*, came out.

Convening Providence & Beyond

As noted earlier, the 2005 conference held in Providence, on the transformation of cities, compared the renaissance of Providence and Liverpool. The aim was to craft fresh questions to guide the unfolding of cities. For three days we engaged in round-table conversations on topics like the aesthetics of place. The only presentations were the opening and closing talks, and we participated in the round-tables to identify the questions that would help cities unfold. No recommendations or action plans. One memorable question we developed: What if we redesigned cities only through the eyes and hearts of children? On Friday Hillman closed the conference with "City, Soul, and Myth." At the end of his talk, people stood and applauded and some were so moved they cried, including me. In that moment I knew this conversation about the city and soul of Providence was just beginning. In the summer of 2005, "Providence & Beyond—an Inquiry into the Future of the City and the Region" was born. A motley crew of 40-50 artists, planners, developers, business owners, activists, and many others met every other month for a morning of conversation. We were progressives, liberals, and conservatives; we were thinkers, doers, and practitioners; we were people from downtown and other neighborhoods. We went forward in the spirit of Roger Williams to inquire about engendering a bold and lively experiment for the soul freedom of all people in the city of Providence.

This was my charge to the Providence & Beyond participants:

> The job of the citizen is to tune the vibration of the city. . . . The Greeks name the city vibration the *polis*—the throng of the people, or the oil that greased the wheels of Athenian democracy. As soul-makers of Providence, it is our work as citizens to "oil this place" to create the conditions that will make the practice of democracy better. The rebirth of Providence is about its people rising up after a long sleepy period of too much introversion. My questions to citizens of Providence: What annoys you about our city? What needs more aesthetic, public attention so we can better breathe in our *polis*? Where will we create the next public places that will serve as the common ground for neighborhoods and ethnic groups to gather, beyond where they now gather alone? Where are we ready to be outrageous? (Leaver, 2005)

In Providence & Beyond, Hillman spoke twice to get the juices flowing. People in the city still say: "I will never forget those talks of James Hillman." In 2008, due to the financial craziness striking the economy and James's patrons leaving Rhode Island, Providence & Beyond took a break and never reconvened (and the reasons for this would be another essay on its own). But for three years, it was an intense community conversation on the culture and soul of Providence. It still ripples in Rhode Island and Connecticut, where one of Hillman's patrons from Providence keeps the conversation going, including the evocation of Hillman's work.

Unfolding what Hillman Wants of Us in Providence and as We Make Cities

In reflecting on editing *City & Soul* and convening Providence & Beyond, Hillman seeded six ideas for city making. These ideas keep me engaged with cities in the region. One, the character of a city is not fixed or formed early as Freud thought it was for people. Hillman helped some important leaders in Providence—who approached Providence like Freud—to see that character of a city unfolds from the seed—the acorn—into its destiny as found in a fully formed oak tree. And this unfolding takes much time. Two, a city has a founding story. Providence's story is of Roger Williams and soul freedom. James loved Williams' irascibility. Three, nature and what most think of as beauty are not found only in the woods. We don't go only to nature for beauty. Cities are natural and full of beauty—go there too. Four, to face difficulties matters more than to find the wind to pull you forward. Five, search for new channels of communication and sources of "the news" beyond the sanctioned ones, especially the sources that bring together people from different walks of life and points of view. Hillman was always stunned by the motley crew of people he engaged with during the city transformation conference and in Providence & Beyond. Six, cities are about preservation and future. Yes, honor the past, but also know when the past is no longer prologue and you step into the future without the focus on preserving the past. Because of this attention paid to Providence, I think my father, if he were alive, would find the city safer today and more to his liking.

I will end with some excerpts from Hillman's "City, Soul, and Myth," which is about why city making is more about seeding the culture to get it to erupt, instead of the usual city approach of building civilization, which is about order, rules, and administration:

> ... the city would turn to poets and chefs, radical visionaries, movie-makers and teachers, and nurses, protesters from sub-cultures, animal proponents, tour guides and fashion designers, curmudgeon traditionalists, nerdy students, and the journeymen who work the streets. . . . Each is a seed of the spontaneous. Each with rebellious critiques and peculiar fantasies that are usually left outside the development of the cities they inhabit. . . . Culture has the possibility of rising up when a handful of people fall in love with each other's ideas. They become drunk and insane with ideas. . . . This moves the culture. In this way we harness the outrage, bridle the objections, and possibly generate fresh surprises. Urbanism and these incredible works of artistry—our society's great cities—cannot be left only to the normally sensibly civilized if the soul of the city is our care—for the soul is not altogether civilized. (2006, p. 402)

Culture has the possibility of rising up

  when a handful of people fall in love

with each other's ideas.

—James Hillman

Robert Romanyshyn, Ph.D., is Professor Emeritus at Pacifica Graduate Institute. He has published six books; contributed essays to numerous edited volumes; has published articles in psychology, philosophy, education, and poetry journals; and has edited special journal issues. He has given lectures and workshops at universities and professional societies in the U.S., Europe, Australia, South Africa, Canada, and New Zealand. He recently finished a new book, *Leaning toward the Poet: Eavesdropping on the Poetry of Everyday Life*, and he is working on a play, "The Frankenstein Prophecy." He lives in Summerland, California, with his wife, Veronica Goodchild.

ROBERT ROMANYSHYN

Sitting on a Bench with James Hillman: Conversations with the Dead

[T]o us he is no more a person
now but a whole climate of opinion

under whom we conduct our different lives:
Like weather he can only hinder or help,
      the proud can still be proud but find it
   a little harder, the tyrant tries to

make do with him but doesn't care for him much:
he quietly surrounds all our habits of growth
      and extends, till the tired in even
   the remotest miserable duchy

have felt the change in their bones and are cheered...

            (Auden, 1976, p. 217)

WHAT W.H. AUDEN SAID in his elegy for Freud in the late 1930s might we also say today of James? Is it not so that James has become a climate of opinion, an atmosphere, the weather of the soul? And, recalling that the poet also said: "The words of a dead man / Are modified in the guts of the living" (Abrams, 1975, p. 2615) might we add that now we are all in the process of digesting and being nourished by James who is now not only atmosphere and climate but also companion, one who shares his subtle bread—soul food—with us, one who though he be absent is still present and who continues to feed the *anima mundi*, the soul of the world of which we are a part?

So we gather today within this atmosphere to continue a conversation with our companion James. The talk this time is about city and soul, about the *polis* and the psyche.

Already this conjunction of city and psyche takes me back to those days in Dallas when Phenomenology and Jungian-Archetypal Psychology irritated each other into breaking the window that had for so long split the public and the private realms. Notwithstanding some disagreements I would have with you, James, regarding your description of mirror and window, your essay "From Mirror to Window: Curing Psychoanalysis of its Narcissism" does recall the co-operation that was necessary between the two traditions (Hillman, 2006). Phenomenology's critique of depth psychology's solipsistic subjectivity—its inveterate narcissistic preoccupation with the patient's interior life—and its return to the things themselves to unravel, as Erwin Straus once noted, the unwritten constitution of everyday life was complemented by archetypal psychology's insistence on the lived world's animation, its liveliness, its image quality, its depth. Together and on the other side of the window, enlivened by the world's breath, inspired by the awful beauty of its sensuous charms, whom did the phenomenologist and archetypal psychologist meet, lingering there, perhaps on a park bench somewhere in Dallas? None other than the poet, patiently waiting to take up the question of an old man, Carl Jung, who quite near the end of his life wondered why his work had to require the death of the poet.

Benches! I like to imagine benches as the strange attractors of soul because, like their physical counterpart, what takes place on benches are conversations that are and remain fluid, dynamic, ongoing; conversations that seek a hint of order in the chaos of experience, which then slips back into that chaos, into what Maurice Merleau-Ponty called the savage being of the world. Every bench, even an empty one, is an oasis in the turbulent currents of life, a place where for a moment one encounters another, be he or she living or dead, a place where the horizons of a past remembered and a future imagined condense in the present into a story, a fable, a way of shaping the stray lines that always undo the fictions we create with our mapmaking minds, a temporary dispensation from the dissolution of the fixed structures we build to endure the continuous descents into the chaos that the alchemy of ordinary life imposes. Benches, even empty ones where the dead, present in their absence, sit and wait, are temporary havens that assuage the loneliness of the road. At the end of this essay I will return to this dynamic quality of benches and their place in the cityscapes of soul. For the moment, however, I see you, James, sitting on a bench with John Keats. Let me eavesdrop for a moment and listen into the conversation:

> *John:* He doubted that he would produce anything but a heap of shards had he made his work aesthetic. He refused therefore to press the poet's wreath upon his head.
>
> *James:* He was right to refuse to do so. Psychology is not poetry and the psychologist is not a poet. And yet something was lost. "Call the world . . . ," you said, "the vale of soul-making. Then you will find out the use of the world."
>
> *John:* The use of the world! What is that use? Indeed, is the world useful? Should it be? And, if it is, then for what and to whom? These are hard questions, especially in your day when so many believe that its use is as resource for your use and abuse.
>
> *James:* I confess that I had to make a decisive turn in my work when I realized that I was reading your words within the context of the

latent virus of narcissism in Jungian and archetypal psychology. The therapy room had isolated itself from nature and the city and had ignored the patient as citizen.

John: And the citizen as patient?

James: That, too, as some of my colleagues in phenomenology had been saying. For them the world is the home and habitat of subjectivity, and for me I had to acknowledge that in considering "the world out there to be useful for making one's own soul," I had made a serious mistake. Psychologists are not poets but with a poetic sensibility one can hear your words as saying "we go through the world for the sake of it's soul making, thereby our own."

(Hillman, 2006, p. 74, emphasis in original)

A breeze scattered the leaves around the bench, and John and James were gone. As I walked around a bend in the road, I was thinking about James's re-visioning of what Keats meant about the world as the vale of soul-making when I saw another bench with a book of poems by Mark Strand lying on it. The breeze of a moment ago had opened the pages to his poem "The Night, The Porch."

> To stare at nothing is to learn by heart
> What all of us will be swept into, and baring oneself
> To the wind is feeling the ungraspable somewhere close by.
> Trees can sway or be still. Day or night can be what they wish.
> What we desire, more than season or weather, is the comfort
> Of being strangers, at least to ourselves. This is the crux
> Of the matter, which is why even now we seem to be waiting
> For something whose appearance would be its vanishing—
> The sound, say,
> Of a few leaves falling, or just one leaf.
> Or less.
> There is no end to what we can learn. The book out there
> Tells us as much, and was never written with us in mind. (1998, p.10)

When we dream we are strangers to ourselves, and just as a dream needs a dream, a poet needs a poet. And there around another twist in the road, John Keats and Mark Strand, the dead and the living, laughing and agreeing that to find out the use of the world one has to lose his or her mind as one has to do if one is to avoid colonizing the dream.

James, might we propose that psychology is useless, or should be (Romanyshyn, 2002)? To find out the use of the world do we not have to let go of the professional temptations to be useful, or meaningful, or even helpful? Are not these so-called values examples of psychology's narcissism, which would replace vernacular understandings of such practices with its professional and prescribed practices?

The days in Dallas when Archetypal Psychology and Phenomenology converged, shattered the window of the Spectator Mind, which, with its eye upon the world, is a disembodied subjectivity that has severed the bonds between the sensuous skin of world and the sensual flesh of the body, a despotic eye that has broken the erotic love affair between them (fig. 3.1).

Figure 3.1. Window as mathematical grid

On the other side of the window, in the chiasm between world and body, we see, as the philosopher Merleau-Ponty says, because we are seeable, to which we might add we speak because we are addressed by the displays of the world. The delightful early morning play of light and shadows (fig. 3.2), or the fading light of a late afternoon that is still dreaming itself as green (fig. 3.3), or the sudden piercing rays of light through a copse of trees (fig. 3.4), or the reflection of clouds not in but as water (fig. 3.5) reveal the splendor in the simple, the extraordinary in the ordinary, and even, if one be inclined to be so bold, the miracle in the mundane. These forays into the world are and should be a key part of any psychological education, an education via their seduction of mind to fall into its flesh.

Earlier I promised I would return to the bench. Now is a good time, for I see a breeze has brought you back. There is a bench up ahead. Let's stop there. I would like to tell you a story about benches to illustrate their place in the chiasm of city and soul.

In the late 1940s and throughout the '50s I grew up in a working-class neighborhood in Brooklyn, New York. In the early evenings of spring, summer, and fall, neighbors would gather after supper to talk and gossip. Those after-dinner rituals enacted mostly by women impressed upon me how those occasions

Figure 3.2. The delightful early morning play of light and shadows

Figure 3.3. The fading light of a late afternoon that is still dreaming itself as green

Figure 3.4. The sudden piercing rays of light through a copse of trees

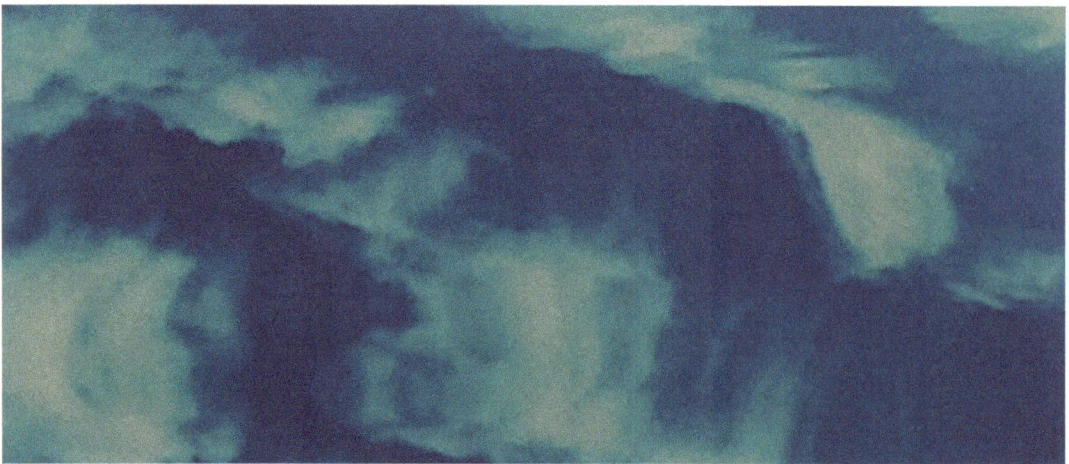

Figure 3.5. The reflection of clouds not in but as water

were forms of consolation, ways in which those women shaped and shared the ordinary struggles and hardships of daily life. Companionship and compassion graced those gatherings. Those benches were places for making communities, places of performance, street theater, neighbors embodied specific types and characters and played out their particular roles. It was, of course, all done without rehearsal, psychological life displayed in action lived out straightforwardly in the world. Witnessing those performances and sometimes eavesdropping on the conversations, I was beguiled by them. They were the grammar school of my vocation into psychology.

Those rituals gradually disappeared as television invaded the neighborhood. The benches emptied as more and more people went inside, in both senses. The characters faded from the world, the bonds of community were broken, and neighbors became strangers.

There were, of course, other kinds of benches where different dramas were enacted. As I got older I gravitated toward the benches where old men gathered. They taught me how to play checkers, chess, poker, and other card games. But sometimes they would just sit there and, with their eyes half closed, they would drift into reverie and tell tall tales as if to no one, reminiscing about their heroic deeds and conquests of women, most of which I learned later were simply melancholic dreams of old men. I liked those moments of tall tales best, but those rituals too disappeared, and their benches became more and more empty.

There is something melancholic about an empty bench (fig. 3.6, 3.7). They are haunted by an absence that is still present. Existing in a kind of liminal space, they shimmer between a thing and an image. Holding a tension between presence

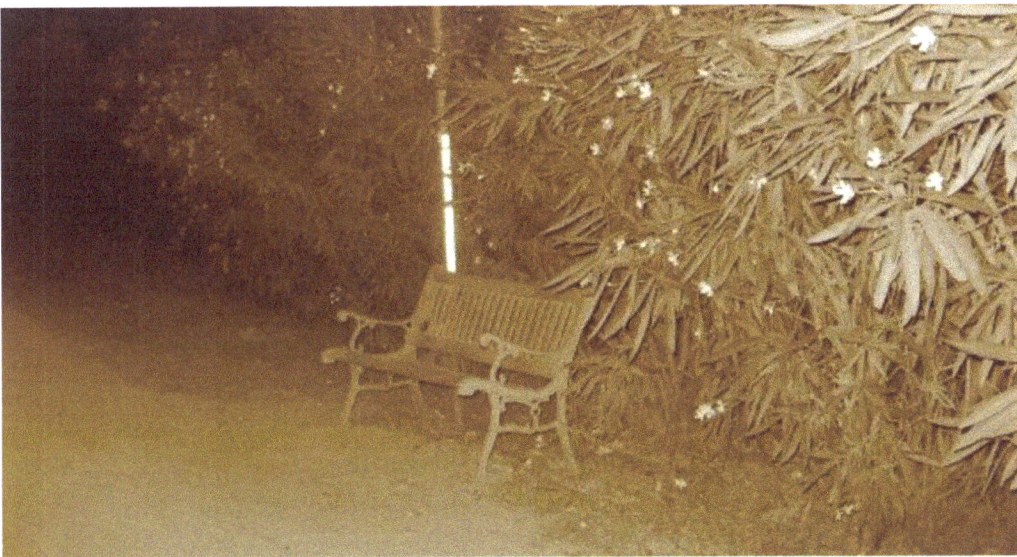

Figure 3.6. There is something melancholic about an empty bench

and absence, they can slow one down, invite one to pause for a moment, to lin-
ger awhile between the certainty of what is—the empty bench—and the uncertainty of what might be—who or what is present in that absence. Not long ago,
James, I had an experience of what might happen when one accepts that subtle
invitation and sits for a moment on an empty bench.

Figure 3.7. Absence in presence

Meeting Patrick Kavanagh in Dublin

Along a walkway near the Liffey River in Dublin, Ireland
is a bench where the Irish poet Patrick Kavanagh used to sit.
I discovered one day that he still sits there,
even though he died many years ago.

'Trying to be a poet,' he told me, 'is a peculiar business.'
'What does it feel like,' I asked, 'to be a poet?'
But then a breeze rustled the leaves in the tree
and he was gone, leaving me with that question.

I have wondered about this business of being a poet for a long time.
I do not think of myself as a poet even though I do write some poems.
And I do read the poets, almost every day, a kind of ritual practice.

But the word itself—poet—it seems to me,
is a benediction bestowed by others.
One does not bless oneself in this way.
Orpheus, the eponymous poet, I think, would be offended.

The tribe of the poets is a small one.
To join it, even if only to tag along at the very far end of their wanderings,
like some beggar,
picking up the crumbs of the feast left by those who are poets,
feels uncomfortable and even dangerous.
Prose feels more comfortable
and I feel more at home in the well-fashioned costumes of my prosaic self.

But sometimes I dream
I am following along at the end of that procession,
wearing a patchwork garment
made by a rag picker from the odds and ends of life.
And the dream always ends on that bench beside the Liffey River in Dublin
where I watch Patrick Kavanagh sewing patches on the sleeves of torn coats.

(Romanyshyn, 2014)

I:3 Sitting on a Bench with James Hillman: Conversations with the Dead

Figure 3.8.

So, James, we are back with the poets. Two psychologists in liminal space! It makes me wonder about the death of the poet that troubled Jung. Is it possible that benches might be places for nurturing a poetic sensibility for a psychology in that liminal space between city and soul? Is it also possible that benches might be places of soul making? If they are, then what might a city without benches be? Soulless?

A final word, James. Benches presume paths. Walking on paths we arrive at benches where the rhythm between movement and rest can change, where one might hesitate between going on and stopping. When there is a bend in the road one might also hesitate for a moment at the uncertainty of the unfamiliar that lies beyond the bend, where the bend with its coy seduction seems to promise some adventure, the possibility of some new wonder (fig. 3.8, 3.9). If benches are the strange attractors of soul making, then might bends in the road be the verbs of soul? Might paths and the bends in paths inscribe in the world the different moods of mind and soul? Might a path in its turning be a place where the straight and narrow road with its clarity and fixed direction, with its tempting promise of progress, embody the indicative mood of life, whereas the turn, suggesting possibility and inviting one to imagine and dream of what might be, might be the subjunctive mood of life? If that be the case, then what might a city be without such paths for going reverse, 'round the bend, and without the benches that line the way?

Figure 3.9.

Figure 3.10.

Postscript:

Dallas! What a place! Thirty-five years ago, soul making took place here. Phenomenology and Archetypal Psychology each following their respective paths from Pittsburgh and Zurich and many places in between to Dallas met each other along the way. A conversation began, often heated as good conversations are, and it continues. James is gone now and yet he lingers. If you pause now and then, you might meet him on an empty bench some morning or evening as you amble and drift along the road in reverie that leads to unexpected places (fig. 3.10).

NOTES

Figure 3.1. is from *Technology as Symptom and Dream* (Romanyshyn, 1989).

Figure 3.2.-3.9. photographs by Robert Romanyshyn.

Figure 3.10. photograph by Veronica Goodchild.

Nor Hall is a writer, theatre artist, and psychotherapist. Author of the chapbook *Traces* and books including *Irons in the Fire, Those Women*, and *The Moon and the Virgin*, Hall writes on a variety of topics inspired by art and artists. She has presented at the Eranos Institute on gender, at the Minneapolis College of Art and Design on Lou Andreas-Salome, and on the Architecture of Intimacy at the Dallas Institute. Dramaturg for the award-winning Archipelago Company in Chapel Hill since 1996, Hall currently enjoys collaborating on performance research projects in the Twin Cities and is an advisor for Pantheatre's Myth and Theatre festival in France. She volunteers at the Center for Victims of Torture, co-chairs the Walker Art Center's Producers Council, and is distracted by thirteen grandchildren.

NOR HALL

What the Foot Wants:
City as Set for Movement Theater

subVERT: *An Interdisciplinary Performance Work*[1]

WE PROVIDE A LINK to the actual video (http://youtu.be/wo6MDYDbIKE), as well as a few stills from the film (below). The reader may also simply follow the unfolding of the text as it explores the imaginal terrain of a fully developed film short. The text supplied is intended to demonstrate the mind work of an archetypally informed dramaturg. Shot in downtown Minneapolis, subVERT was shown in a theater as if it were a dance performance. Working with a live feed, the directors incorporated actual sound and movement made by the dancer from outside the theater while the film was being shown. At a critical juncture, the dancer herself entered the stage, crawling out from under a Siren's bird foot on screen.

'Subvert,' to overthrow something established or existing, a performance work conceived and designed to explore and subvert expectations of space, dance, audience, self, and city.[2]

> Hear the voice of the bard . . .
> Whose ears have heard
> The Holy Word,
> That walk'd among the ancient trees,
>
> Calling the lapsed Soul,
> And weeping in the evening dew:
> That might control,
> The starry pole;
> And fallen, fallen light renew!
> (Blake, 1794)

"Debbie" the dancer, who is supposed to dance after all, is caught between her own characters Star Dust and Dark Matter and driven to subvert the choreographed dance-on-stage imperative by singing instead. Rather than coming out of the wings to dance, she comes out of a film to sing. Instead of a new piece showcasing her reliably beautiful moves, she is filmed—heard off-stage in live feed—trying to get through a series of baffling obstacles and fears to emerge as the one who can make her dream audible.

The gods appear in our disorders, public and private.

With regard to not confining analysis to human subjectivity (Hillman, 2004, p. 67), subVERT works with the psyche of the dancer and of dance itself to loosen it from the hold of the stage performance. Instead of dancer-like moves of the limbs on a lit stage before a seated audience, the character allows in awkwardness (dislocation, dismemberment) as well as vocalization, film, and "the outside." Outside and inside reverse. Sounds of nature (cicadas) emerge from the building. Sounds of the city (sirens) enter into the building. The stage set widens to include city street, sidewalk, roof, exit doors to the outside, building corridors, bathroom stalls, and only includes the actual theater at the end of the performance.

Southern Theater, a JH story

Instead of the proverbial American "Go West, young man," I was told "Go South, young woman." At "Echo's Subtle Body" in 1979, I told James Hillman that I'd achieved my dream to go to Zurich and study and to be in analysis with Marie-Louise von Franz ("tourist trade," she called it), and that I was going to take a long weekend in November to go down to Pompeii to spend some time in the Villa of Mysteries. He said I had it backward: better go South to Italy for the fall and take one long weekend up North to see von Franz.

It was in the lobby of Minneapolis' Southern Theater ten years later—after seeing a New York Creation Company's production of Camillo's Memory Theater[3]—I felt the naïve overwhelm of "wanting to be a dramaturg" with no idea what it was.

Process

Eventually, going South, into the body and into a collective body of imagination—resulted in climbing onto an invisible, shared, trustworthy scaffold constructed simply by the choice to collaborate. In yearning to work together, to labor together—we create an internal labor force, collaborating artists as employees of the imagination.[4] What is found there comes after the fact. For example, these visual and aural images—researched and reached into for their depth and direction—first came from discussions between the artistic director and the dancer in the form of a simple dream-like narrative.[5] After that, the layering.

STREET
The SOUTHERN
SIREN
SIDEWALK

PURSE
FOOT
MAIL SLOT
BENCH
SHOE
BIRDFOOT
TOILET STALL
CHILD/HOMUNCULUS
DREAM/SONG
CICADAS
SEATBELT
STORM ALERT
CHAINSAW
MARQUEE LIGHTS
DOOR

i.e., FOOT

The cautious matrons from Minnetonka or Plano can be overheard to say "I wouldn't set foot in the city," fearing the traffic, problems with parking, the heart-stopping sirens and what they imply. Putting your foot in the water, or merely sticking your toe in, is to get the measure of a place and a moment, almost a commitment, on the way to jumping in feet first. Then there's no way out as we recall from the indelible foot piercing the membrane of the frieze in the Villa of Mysteries when the terrified initiate wants out. The ancient *numpere* (umpire, 800 BCE) knows you are in. The barefoot bards stomping the perimeter of holy ground set the stage in motion: "And there rose up the chosen public umpires, nine in all, and they made smooth the dancing ground (*choros*) and wide the meeting place (*agon*). The youth rose up, skilled in dancing and they beat the divine floor with their feet . . . and only then did the poet touch his harp and sing" (Murray, 1927, p. 30). We see Debbie (not dressed for walking) in the city on the verge of meeting the *tremendum*—a tremendous confrontation with the other side (Dark Matter) that will change her. She hits the interior wall and would turn—even to pivot like the initiate.

Straddling worlds, one is orphaned or singled out, a *monosandalos* or single-sandaled, like gods and heroes with a foot in each world (Hecate Monosandalos)—one shoe off and one shoe on—limping across the fields with Hecate, or tearing through the backstage corridor after an encounter with the Siren. "Diddle diddle dumpling my son John, one shoe off and one shoe on."

The naked foot was blessed by the Muses who trod in circular iambic pentameter around a wellspring. A severed foot (= a votive limb like a milagro) could be taken to the healing sanctuary (Southern Theater bathroom as Aesclepion) where soothing water washed through the propitiate's dream chamber might aid reflection on the disaster of being cut off from the source of inspiration (fig. 4.1). A city that offers no walking is also a city that offers no dwelling for the mind: "With the soul-calming language of walking, the dartings of the mind begin to form into a direction" (Hillman, 2006, p. 253). Darting of Debbie's blank eyes, heart pounding, siren declaring emergency. "There is probably an archetypal cure going on in walking, something profoundly affecting the mythical substrata of our lives. When we are most in the grip of anxiety, as in nightmares, we are often unable to move our legs" (p. 253).

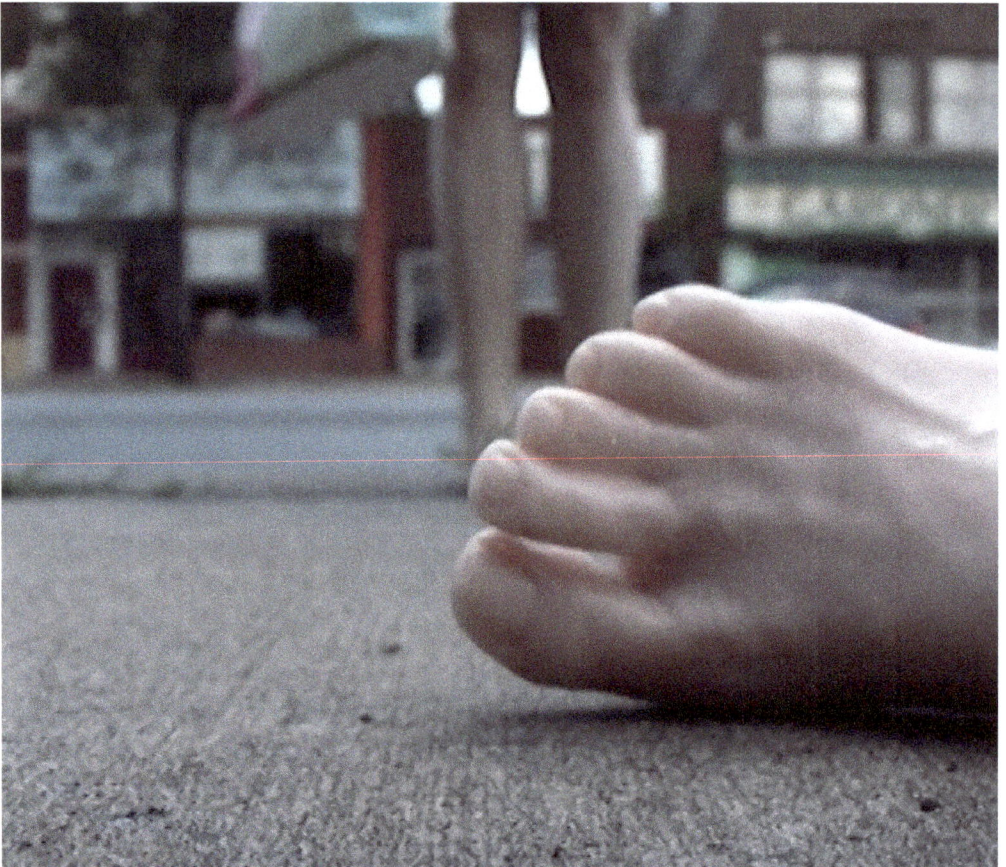

Figure. 4.1 Still of severed foot, subVERT, 2011. Retrieved from http://youtu.be/wo6MDYDbIKEA.

In panic, we run toward that which we fear (Hillman, 2007 [fig. 4.2]).

Debbie ingesting cicadas (tattle-tales to the Muses), resisting the nightmare. Storm coming. Fastening seatbelts, legs unable to move. "In dreams, I walk with you..." (Roy Orbison, 1963). Improbable traversing of corridor to back stage door to confront Siren Dark Matter (played by herself) who has locked the door to performance.

Figure 4.2 Still of Debbie running toward Southern Theater, subVERT, 2011. Retrieved from http://youtu.be/wo6MDYDbIKE.

"Walking also brings me in contact with my animal nature" (Hillman, 2006, p. 253). Debbie getting out from under the foot of the controlling Siren fell foot first through the violent birth hole. As if drawn out the same way she went in (visionary cult practice of Zeus Trophonius). Deliteralizing the personal. The Siren couldn't walk—only flex her birdfoot in the air and scream.

Instead of the missing foot in her purse she finds the means to send out her voice. Brings the song to the audience (who had been expecting "dance"). Big deal for Debbie. Once she finds her voice she moves humanly, as a natural animal woman, again, rather than a stilted "ditz." Big door opens back out into the city. In the actual performance she goes through it.

"When we can . . . embark on a more circular, indirect approach. . . . Walking takes on the movement of soul" (Hillman, 2006, p. 255).

There's a kind of compression of our humanness in the city. Navigating the sidewalks, streets, skyways, crosswalks, building entrances and exits—we are in it together. In something of our own construction that reflects our states of being (so described by Hillman). Site-specific theater work invites the eye to wander in these places while the body, step by step, follows through warehouse expanses, down alleys, in and out of storefronts, or up into rafters taking in meaning idiosyncratically and "cellularly" through the body's pace. *subVERT* is unusual in this regard because the audience is actually seated in a theater. They watch the film at first, expectation subverted, but then the eye is distracted by sounds coming from the corridor immediately adjoining the theater. As Debbie bumps along to "In Dreams" she bangs on doors with her body and her bag, issuing an ultimate final scream that identifies her with the sequined Siren in the wings. Still seated, the audience follows her emergence as a sort of torchlight singer (fig. 4.3) —and have to squish together and move their knees or stand as she climbs over them into their midst to finish her dark lullaby before actually directing their ears and gaze back into the immediate city night.

Figure 4.3 Still of Debbie in the spotlight, subVERT, 2011. Retrieved from http://youtu.be/wo6MDYDbIKE.

When we can . . .

embark on a more circular,

indirect approach. . . .

Walking takes on the movement of soul.

—James Hillman

NOTES

[1] *subVERT* was produced independently in 2011 and funded, in part, by a grant from the McKnight Foundation.

[2] My collaborators are devoted to articulating the poetic basis of mind by way of body moves, gestural vocabulary, and image and sound production. In this case, the process was led by Shawn McConneloug, artistic director of Orchestra, a nationally recognized movement/theatre company, and included cinemaphotographer/editor Andrew Welken with McKnight dance award recipient Mary Ann Bradley and composer/cellist Chris Lancaster. I served as research dramaturg.

[3] See *The Memory Theatre of Giulio Camillo* by Matthew Maguire (1986): http://www.creationproduction.org/maguire/pdf/memorytheatre_mmaguire.pdf.

[4] On the collaborative working process, how image comes first in devising, see my "Vanishing Writing" in *The Open Page*, No. 6 (March 2001). (http://www.odinteatret.dk/books--film/the-open-page/no-6---text.aspx).

[5] See Shawn McConneloug of The Gymnasium (http://www.thegymtc.com/#/shawn-mcconneloug/4574890083), a consortium of creative risk-takers in search of good ideas and new connections. McConneloug is an interdisciplinary artist whose first language is movement. Her current research explores the creative intersection between dance and neuroscience.

With the soul-calming

language of walking,

the dartings of the mind

begin to form into a direction.

—James Hillman

PART II:

PATIENT AS CITIZEN

Gustavo Beck is professor of Psychology at Universidad Iberoamericana in Mexico City, where he also graduated, as well as a translator of books and essays on psychology and the humanities, and a clinical psychologist with a private practice in Mexico City. He received a M.A. degree in Mythological Studies from Pacifica Graduate Institute, in Santa Barbara, California, where he is currently a Ph.D. candidate. His dissertation is an in-depth reading of James Hillman's *Re-visioning Psychology*. He trained in depth/archetypal psychology at the Instituto de Psicología Profunda en México (Institute for Depth Psychology in Mexico), where he currently teaches and serves as a clinical supervisor. His interests revolve essentially around archetypal theory, particularly regarding its impact over contemporary social, cultural, and political issues. He is a co-founder of and contributor to the *Journal of Archetypal Studies*, which was created in order to foster a broader and more critical conversation around the ideas presented by archetypal theory.

GUSTAVO BECK

Returning to the Soul's Body Politic:
Reflections Toward an Imaginal Democracy

Hence to rework our notion of psychic reality implicates each of us in reworking our background, the tradition which continues to feed our theory-forming and our idea of reality.

—James Hillman (2006), "*Anima Mundi:* Return of the Soul to the World," p. 48

I STAND BEFORE YOU today with more intentions in mind than I can possibly handle. I intend to speak about psychology. I intend to speak about politics. I intend (and this is more difficult) to speak about psychology and politics simultaneously. I intend (and this is even more difficult) to speak psychologically about politics and politically about psychology. To continue my self-destruction spree, I intend to perform my inquiry through the specific notions of image and of democracy in terms of archetypal psychology, in general, and of James Hillman's work in particular. Finally, most important and in order to push this professional suicide to a limit, I intend today to betray James Hillman: I intend to speak against his writings in this forum that is aimed at honoring them. I intend to do so, of course, for the sake of psychology and politics; and in my defense, I am fully committed to fulfill my betrayal as imaginally and as democratically as I possibly can.

Before I stab my teacher in the back, however, I will provide some context. To do so I ask two very simple, but impossible, double questions: what does it mean to speak psychologically, and what does it mean to speak politically? My chosen corollary is equally ridiculous: what does it mean to speak imaginally, and what does it mean to speak democratically? It seems unlikely that anyone who studies either imagination or democracy seriously would venture a definitive answer to such a question. My proposition here, however, is that even if we have no clear idea about what imagination or democracy are, it is possible to contend that these two perspectives are intertwined and manifest two sides of the same coin: to speak imaginally is to speak democratically, and to speak democratically is to speak imaginally. The task here (other than assaulting Hillman), then, is to use image and democracy to give body to the two-way bridge between the psychological and the political.

Here I will postpone my treason and grant James Hillman this much: he fundamentally agreed with all that I have said so far. In fact, he articulated it with much more skill. That the psychological is political is also his vision. Hillman (2006) spoke about how depth psychology has traditionally neglected politics. According to him, "this lacuna indicates the presence of denial, a defense mechanism against the political, keeping analytical psychotherapy immune from infection by the body politic" (p. 51). This denial, Hillman argues, is based upon several assumptions, among them that "the political is not psychological and the psychological is not political" (p. 52). Thus far, the betrayer agrees with the soon-to-be-betrayed. But let us follow Hillman's wording and formulate a question: what does it mean—and what does it imply—to be "infect[ed] by the body politic"?

Something else I am obliged to concede to James Hillman: he was a democratic writer. Few authors understand as deeply as he did the degree up to which psychology and politics imply each other. In his texts, myriads images spoke, each conveying their own messages with their own voices. His books were populated by ideas that, much like persons, supported each other and fought with each other. As if in a congressional debate, Hillman's pages are constantly speaking among themselves, arguing, pushing, yielding, dissenting, persuading, and (yes, let us admit it) betraying each other. It is this textual democracy that keeps Hillman's writing imaginally alive. Throughout his career, Hillman constantly advocated in favor of allowing the multiple, personified voices of the psyche to speak. Also, by venturing into various themes, disciplines, and fields that had thus far remained foreign to psychological inquiry, Hillman contributed greatly to what we could call a project on the democratization of psychology—which implied both promoting the entry of psychology into realms that were considered unpsychological and allowing the entrance of new modes of constructing reality into psychology's own rigid structures of thought. Hillman's work was, in many ways, an attempt to open the world to the multiple voices of psychology, and to open psychology to the multiple voices of the world.

This is one first move that should be acknowledged in Hillman's exploration of image and democracy: he interiorized politics. This move is based in a fundamental trait that, according to archetypal psychology, is shared by the imaginal and the democratic: multiplicity. Hillman, in his incessant argument in favor of personified polytheism, is implicitly also supporting a plural vision that is, at least in theory, essential to democracy. In a polytheistic pantheon, every god personifies a valid archetypal stance, and it is these stances that back up the multiplicity of visions that manifest in each citizen of the *polis*. "*Polis* always reflects psyche in both classical and modern democracies," he said in *The Myth of Analysis* (1998, p. 154). In other words, each and every one of us is a city, a political body. In *Re-Visioning Psychology* (1975), making a case for Jung's archetypal persons and attacking what he calls Freud's "imperialistic fantasy," he establishes what could be understood as a very political, and democratic, conception of personality: "Rather than a field of forces, we are each a field of internal personal relationships, an interior commune, a body politic" (pp. 22, 26).

Hillman was not only a restless democratic writer, he was also a profoundly psychological democrat. He was radical in his contribution to a political understanding of personality, which naturally flows into an imaginal understanding of democracy. Our individual selves are built in the same way that a democracy is: we are inhabited by multiple, differing visions, and these visions are in constant conflict—our personalities are "field[s] of internal relationships" and our identities are "interior commune[s]." You are not only you, and I am not only myself. We are not just one person; each of us is, in fact, many persons at once. Furthermore, each of us is a body politic inhabited by archetypal presences who often disagree among themselves, and who possibly frequently do not even like each other. Our neurotic, personal conflicts are something like an inner version of a senatorial hearing or a town hall meeting. Our lives are intimately political: different archetypal presences manifest through our complexes, and our personality is the product not so much of who wins or who loses the argument, but rather of the permanent tension between the different visions that live within our psychic structure.

In this wonderful and radical scenario, it becomes impossible to say unequivocally "who we are." The only way to define us here is in terms of our psychic struggles and our inner quarrels. Much like our governments, we are always at odds with ourselves, questioning ourselves, fighting with ourselves. In an ideal situation, such tension is creative; but usually, again like with our governments, our inner divisions turn our personalities into quite an inefficient instrument. We are unable to make up our minds, end up with only partial resolutions, and modify our entire public policy as quickly as Henry VIII changed wives. As early as 1967 Hillman said, "Problems in psychology are not something people have, but something people are" (*Insearch*, p. 30). Our personalities are nothing but never-ending discussions among the members of our body politic. But a curse comes with democracy: a truly democratic body politic must be open to voices that conflict with one another, and that sometimes see as their mission to exterminate the other. To borrow the words of Mexican poet and essayist Octavio Paz (2014), democratic republics are "breeding grounds for envy and demagogy," whose "endemic disease[s are] civil dissensions and the struggle between factions" (p. 210).

What I have described so far is radical psychology: each of us is a city. Let us complicate it further by examining what is radically political in Hillman: each of us, as city, reflects and interacts with actual, outer, specific cities. Imaginal democracy becomes more complex when we take into account that it is a two-way street. Hillman (2006) again: "If Self and its draw toward reflective interiority . . . is constituted of communal contingencies, then the draw toward interiority must at the same time be a draw toward exteriority, toward the contingencies of the actual ecological field" (p. 60). This is, of course, Hillman arguing in favor of his psychology of extraversion. In his view, psychology underpins narcissistic patterns that impede the body politic and its energy from flowing from our inner lives into the outer world. It becomes crucial, therefore, to become aware that our own, let us say personal, body politic is in constant interaction with another body politic, essentially the body politic that is the outer world. Our inner democracies mirror actual democratic systems and political dynamics.

This is Hillman's second vital move for the sake of imagination and politics: he exteriorized psychology. We are all, as individuals, polyvalent and bubbling cities, but these apparently subjective political bodies engage constantly with actual, outer cities that contain us. We have then cities within cities. With this incredibly complex argument Hillman opened a window and threw our discipline out there, into the world—into the *polis*. "For patient to become citizen," he says, "analytical psychotherapy can hardly do more at first than return to the world the emotions which call the patient to the world" (2006, p. 61). His essential claim is that emotions are not private property; they belong to the world, to community, and to soul. It can hardly get more political, and psychological, than this. Hillman invites us to "go straight through the window into the world. . . .

Let us imagine . . . *the world itself as psychoanalyst showing us soul*, showing us how to be in it soulfully" (p. 75, emphasis in original).

This proposition inverts the entire equation both for politics and for psychology. We now learn that politics are subject to emotional and imaginal experience, and that psychology is subject to public, democratic discussion.

This builds a sufficiently solid two-way bridge between psychology and politics. But it is not enough. And although my intentions with this essay are too many, I have not forgotten about the betrayal part. So this is where I will backstab Hillman. However, since I respect Hillman, I wish to backstab him frontally. In order to do this, as I said before, I am going to use the most democratic weapon I can come up with at the moment: Hillman himself. My dagger is Hillman's work. I am going to be a true student of Hillman, and use Hillman's words against Hillman. Because I respect his writing, it is my psychological and political responsibility to betray his writing. That said, allow me to attack.

I propose a reflexive exercise: let us imagine Hillman's work as a city. I want us, for a moment, to imagine his writing as a body politic. Who inhabits this city? What are its demographics and its neighborhoods? What are its usual activities? How does the city move? What do people eat in this city? What are its public policies like? What are its hierarchies, its social and its economic divides? Who are its authorities? Who is its mayor? Who governs? Better yet: who really governs? What is our political system like? Are we a democracy? Do we have a congress? How many parties does our system have? How representative are the visions of those parties of the general population? What are our interior and exterior policies? How does this city handle crises and social unrest? How does it cope with conflict? How does law enforcement work? Who are our police force and our attorney general? What's the crime rate? What is the most common crime here? What is the murder rate? Who is most frequently murdered in our city? What are our jails like? Where are the homeless in our city? Does this city import or export inhabitants? Where are our immigrants? Where are our exiles? Where are our poor? Who has been forgotten?

Furthermore, and if we are truly psychological and political about it, how does Hillman's work as a city relate to other cities? How does its body politic relate to that complex cluster of cities: to the city of history, or philosophy, or physics, or sociology, or anthropology, or religion? How able are our diplomats or our armies when we engage with the cities of Foucault, Marx, Hegel, Freud, Jung, Žižek, Badiou, Strathern, Sahlins, or Chomsky? Most important, how does this city engage with those other strange creatures: actual, literal cities—not only with Dallas, Zürich, Thompson, Santa Barbara, Mexico City, or São Paulo, but also Crimea, Gaza, Jerusalem, Havana, Caracas, or any city in West Africa facing the attack of the Ebola virus?

All these questions do not play against Hillman's work because they are mostly questions that he either asked or that can be derived from his work. They do play against his work in another sense, however, because the answers he provided for them are either insufficient or non-existent. What I am doing here, essentially, is accusing Hillman of not being Hillmanian enough, of not following his argument through and of stopping the movement of his writing's body politic in certain places.

That this happened, however, is understandable. It was impossible for Hillman to examine his body politic in this way. Hillman was busy building a city; it would be unfair to ask him to rebuild it himself. That is up to those of us who consider ourselves to be somehow inhabitants of, or related to, such city.

Therefore, my attack against Hillman is really an attack against myself. If I am a citizen of this city, it is my job to work these questions out, to work out the theory's body politic. If I want to be psychologically and politically honest, I have to share my vision with you, fellow citizens, and listen to your own impression of where our city stands. My vision is that this city is in urgent need of work. We need to rethink its buildings, its streets and its avenues, its monuments, its education system, and its constitution. Also I have a feeling that our sewage system is in desperate need of cleansing. I also think—and the fact that I waited to come to the Dallas Institute to say this is only testament to my own tendencies towards professional suicide—that one of the first buildings that has to be remodeled, if not torn down, is Hillman's "Return to Greece" and his positions with regards to the metaphorical aspects of soul.

I will not argue in this paper why this is the case, on the one hand because I have no time for it, on the other, because we have all the time in the world for it. At least for me, this is the moment to name our city's needs. We will have time to address them, one by one. Imagination is democratic, so everyone will have time to speak and to act, many times. Our theory, like ourselves, is nothing but a never-ending discussion (a dance of sorts) among people who mostly disagree with each other. As I said at the start, this essay contains more intentions than it can handle. But in a way this is how democracy and imagination work: they are the condition of having too many intentions, followed by the responsibility of putting those intentions out there, followed by the humility of shutting up and standing still, followed by the loving act of listening to others reacting to your intentions, followed by the patient practice of allowing the intentions to be transformed by such reactions, followed by the respectful discipline of responding, yet again, with new intentions. This infection by the body politic, as Hillman describes it, is (at least for this modest citizen) the spirit behind imaginal and democratic speech, thought, and practice.

At this point, however, I am walking into that phase of the imaginal-democratic circle when one shuts up. And so I shall.

Hence to rework our notion of psychic

reality implicates each of us

in reworking our background,

the tradition which continues to feed

our theory-forming and our idea of reality.

—James Hillman

Randolph Severson, Ph.D., is a family therapist and writer whose books include: *Spiritual Existential Counseling; A Catholic Soul Psychology; Adoption: Philosophy and Experience; The Soul of Family Preservation*; and *Adoption: Charms and Rituals for Healing*. Nominated by Congressman Joe Barton, he received the Congressional Angel of Adoption. He was also a Recipient of the Baran-Pannor Award for Excellence in Adoption.

RANDOLPH SEVERSON

The Dailiest Day

THE CITY, THE GREATNESS, the grandeur, the loveliness, the splendor. The glory that was Greece, the grandeur that was Rome. Art, culture, excitement, music, fine cuisine, high finance and commerce, bicycle paths and walking trails, high speed public transportation, green spaces, sparkling fountains, gleaming pools.

The postmodern age is the Age of the City, a true Renaissance of the City. It is difficult to travel anywhere in America now, to any once-great city that may have fallen on hard times and not be astonished at the transformation, especially with respect to culture and the arts—new museums, symphony halls, restaurants, music venues—more human-scaled living, working, and shopping. Downtown no longer a dead zone, but a hot spot with a heartbeat, the center of the action after dark and after hours, as well as during the day.

What is happening everywhere is a re-emergence of the City-State, an organization and a celebration of human life reminiscent of ancient Greece and Renaissance Italy.

To my mind, no single voice and vision in the last half century is more eloquent, descriptive, evocative, far-seeing, discerning, and insightful about the Age that we have entered into, the Age of the City and the Citizen—of Patient as Citizen—than James Hillman's. But he wasn't just a voice and vision, he was a participant, a Citizen, and through his time here in Dallas, in terms he would detest, a Mover and a Shaker. Dallas is what it is today, in part, because of James Hillman, his voice and vision, and of course his inspiration, but also because of his leadership—a leadership typically expressed collegially, with a warm chuckle and a piquant aside.

Hillman didn't just ride the wave of the New Urbanism; he steered it. History, if we believe in something like a *zeitgeist,* a change in the Collective Mind, may ultimately say "he was at the helm." Of course, he had his predecessors— Lewis Mumford, Jane Jacobs, William Whyte. But Hillman was in Dallas in the '70s—"Did you ever see Dallas from a DC-9 at night?" (that's Jimmy Dale Gilmore in 1972). "Dallas is a beautiful woman . . . a woman who will walk on you when you're down." Dallas, right time, right place, a *kairos*, Psyche in the City, Aphrodite, too. The television show, with JR and Bobby, an international sensation, premiered in 1978, the year Hillman delivered his ground-breaking essay, "City and Soul."

So how to serve this city? How to be a citizen in all the fullness, richness, pride, and glory of that term? *Civis Urbanus Sum.* This is the focus of the essays gathered in volume two of the *Uniform Edition, City & Soul*, which oriented much of Hillman's work in later years. The key, radical idea is the notion of the soul, the self, as *interiorization of the community*. We are *not* such stuff as dreams are made of but of our surroundings, our cities, and our communities. Hillman was harkening back to the old idea that "there is nothing in the mind that was not first in the senses." We are what we eat, what we taste and see, what we touch, what we smell, what we hear. We are sentient creatures: the keener the senses, the more attuned the ear; the subtler the touch, the more we are like animals, our companions in creation, models, not mascots, the more alive we'll be. To know thyself means to know thy surroundings, to know them the way an animal does, an artist, a politician, a historian, to know how to survive there—main street, back street, side street, streets not on any map—to nose around, to walk around, to ride the train and bus, to get around town, to glory in the energy and beauty of it, the freshness of the morning cup of coffee, the delicious aromas of restaurant row, the sudden radiances, the Venusian epiphanies; and the darkness, too, the projects, slums, shelters, the furniture and cars in the yard, the abandoned buildings, boarded-up windows, the liquor stores; the famous crimes, the sixth floor window, the ghosts who haunt; and to get to know the people, mingle in the crowds, the neighbors, the movers and the shakers, the issues of the day, whether it be by following the market on your phone or reading the newspaper, attending meetings, fundraisers, cocktail parties, conferences, "get up, stand up, stand up for your rights;" and learn the history of person, place and thing, old files, old books, old papers, old stories, old people, whether on the web or at the library, to dig down deep in it, to delve in all its dirt; and to marvel at it, too, the genius, sacrifice, corruption, and heroism that made and makes any city great.

Now let me pause to clarify. I'm not a closet Aristotelian. Or only one part so. The other three parts are Blakean, Coleridgean, and High Romantic. Blake declared that to see a World in a grain of sand, the Heavenly in the Earthly City, the air, the literal air, which, of course, is always more than literal. It is "awash with Angels" (Wilbur, 2004), "the Blessed Virgin compared to the air we breathe" (Hopkins, 1918). To return soul to the senses and sense to the soul, so that "coming to our senses" connotes both the density and textures of the perceptual realm together with a psychological and spiritual awakening. The literal always more than literal. Merleau-Ponty would have called it the Chiasm, that inspiration and expiration of Being.

This, or some near version of it, is how one becomes a citizen, whether in Athens or Venice, Paris, or Dallas. And a therapy that seeks to engender, enliven, encourage, and embolden citizenship—a "coming to your senses," "*sensus communis*," "facts of life" kind of therapy—is a therapy that, first, tries to get people to notice, to notice all the facts of their surroundings; first, an inventory of sensory delights and pleasures—"Some are born to sweet delight" as Blake wrote.

To notice and, then, to *feel*. But feeling in the Hillman sense of valuing, of tasting, of developing a kind of refined, differentiated, and knowledgeable taste whose opposite is tasteless, tactless, tacky, ignorant, no nothing, no imagination. Know what you like; and then slow it down, enjoy and savor it—*event becomes experience*. So much distress and so much dysfunction—schizophrenia, schizoid personality disorder, depression, social anxiety, Henry Miller's *Air Conditioned Nightmare* in which we all abide—is characterized by anhedonia, that is, senseless suffering, or else the sensory onslaught of bipolar, ADHD, or A-Spectrum disorders. Change, then—*change* as soul-making, as urban soul-making, as an education in citizenship—becomes both relatively easy and a lifelong task. It can be short term, a single encounter, even, or like classical analysis or Bowenian family therapy, it can go on forever. If you don't like the way you are, the way you feel, the way other people are treating you, change it, *change your surroundings*, the surroundings which the counseling conversation takes great time and pains to encourage the patient to notice. If the Self is the interiorization of the Community, the community of people, places, and things amid which you dwell, then change the community, a little at a time. Start with things: your bed and bath, mealtimes, furniture, ritualized routines; move on to places: get out, see and be seen, find a place, a spot where you feel anonymous—that's fine, maybe even preferable—but be alive, vital, where you feel in the swing, the swim, a part of things, the noise and hustle bustle buoying you, city sights and sounds as soul food—and frequent it; move on to people: to Church, to politics. Ask yourself what gets the best out of you? What enlivens, encourages, and emboldens you? What do you feel called by? And, short of that, where do you think you might be needed, could lend a hand, could serve and contribute: write a Letter to the Editor; join a choir, a book club, a sports league, Big Brother/Big Sister, Soup Kitchen, Helping Hands, Reading for the Blind; pick up litter, go to a precinct meeting. Travel. Change your world; you change yourself. Everything gets better. As Hillman suggests: "*. . . the draw toward interiority must at the same time be a draw toward exteriority, toward the contingencies of the actual ecological field—where I am placed, with whom I am, what is happening with my animals, my food, my furniture and what the toaster, the newspaper and the refrigerator's purr do in the field I am in*" (2006, p. 60, my emphasis).

I say change is easy; it is easy in therapy—providing that the therapist has enough persuasiveness, or *ethos, pathos,* and *logos*—that is, character, tact, and sound reasoning—and the client enough courage, enough grit and zest, to embark on this kind of urban adventure. But that's one role of the therapist (isn't it?), to persuade, to embolden, and inspire. For Alfred Adler it was encouragement to Social Interest, which already in 1914 he called an "aesthetic exercise." I call it *commissioning a quest*—an odyssey, part civics lesson, part urban survival course, part Weekend Guide "O Taste and See," whose object is pride, Civic Pride, the pride that echoes down the centuries: Athens, Florence, Venice, Rome, Vienna, London, Paris, Prague, Berlin, New York, Chicago. *Civis Urbanus Sum*.

So that's the goal, then, Civic Pride, Civic Identity, *Civis Urbanus Sum*, which must serve as the goal of any true Renaissance psychology, and which is (I think) the most, echoing Suzanne K. Langer (1967), "fecund" way of describing James Hillman's life's work, a psychology as much Machiavelli and Medici as Bruno and Ficino, as much Thomas Jefferson, who, as McLuhan (2011) so perceptively observed was "a virtuoso of the Italian Renaissance in eighteenth-century dress"—as Jung. In his puer *fantasia* Hillman's exemplar, his beau ideal, was Odysseus who, over the course of many decades and the famous turn to the world, became an urbanized Odysseus in Joyce's *Ulysses* (1986), Leopold Bloom; and a Hillmanian Renaissance therapy is always a Day in the Life, the Dailiest Day, a therapy of 16 June 1904, a therapy of urbanity and worldliness, of slapstick humor and sensory delight, of archetypal depth and picaresque affirmation—and the last word on Hillman, the last words of Joyce's great novel, of Molly Bloom, with their faint echo of the Marion response to that "Angel of reality / seen for a moment / standing in the door" (Stevens, 1990, p. 496): "Yes," she says, "I said yes I will. Yes" (p. 644).

Some are born to sweet delight.

—William Blake

Mary Watkins, Ph.D., is co-founder of the Community Psychology, Liberation Psychology, and Ecopsychology Specialization in the M.A./Ph.D. Depth Psychology Program, Pacifica Graduate Institute. She is co-author of *Toward Psychologies of Liberation, Up Against the Wall: Re-Imaging the U.S.-Mexico Border*, and *Talking With Young Children About Adoption*, author of *Waking Dreams and Invisible Guests: The Development of Imaginal Dialogues*, co-editor of *Psychology and the Promotion of Peace*, and a participatory research team member of In the Shadows of Paradise: Testimonies from the Undocumented Immigrant Community in Santa Barbara. She works at the interfaces between Euro-American depth psychologies and psychologies of liberation from Latin America, Africa, North America, and Asia, promoting peacebuilding and social and environmental justice through the teaching and practicing of critical, dialogical, and participatory approaches.

MARY WATKINS

Capitalism and the Commons

IN 2010, JAMES HILLMAN and I began to talk about the possibility of hosting a conference on capitalism at Pacifica Graduate Institute. Sadly, it was not to be. I have welcomed this timely invitation to review his writings in search of his ideas about capitalism. As the millennium turned, it was becoming ever clearer to both of us that late neoliberal globalized capitalism was shaping both our cities and our souls. In his 1997 essay "Farewell to Welfare" (in Leaver, 2006), Hillman says, "Unbridled late-stage capitalism euphemistically called a 'free-market economy' aims in one direction only. It is single-mindedly obsessed with growth of profit, which throws the shadow of depression into society as downsizing, pink slips, expansion of debt, and bankruptcies" (p. 376).

This single-minded pursuit of ever-greater profits causes what could be called a modern day "enclosure of the commons" in American cities.[1] In cities deemed "successful," older established neighborhoods of color have been riddled by gentrification, creating distant peripheries of people torn from their roots, marooned from work opportunities and needed transportation. City blocks—once home to distinctive and varied businesses—are now possessed and homogenized by the financial sector or megachain corporations. The failure to think regionally has left some neighborhoods suffering the "slow violence" (Nixon, 2011) of environmental pollution, while others become eco-exemplary (Pavel & Anthony, 2009). In failed cities, acres of ghost blocks prevail. Citizens in bankrupt cities like Camden, New Jersey are abandoned to gather their subsistence by dismantling their own vacant buildings to sell scrap metal to China (Hedges & Sacco, 2014). Seventy-five percent of their failing city budget is for police and fire—most often securitization, not *for* its citizens but in effect *against* them. Such self-cannibalization is an end stage of late capitalism, where even in the heart of the global system, in the U.S., the common good is sacrificed to a growing, tense polarity of unimaginable profit on one side and bare survival on the other.

Excess greed operates like a viral monocrop in the psyche, forcing out the empathy, compassion, and conscience that are necessary for the self-restraint that contributes to the common good, and the differentiated emotions of shame, sorrow, guilt, and outrage upon which they depend. For the dispossessed, economic insecurity and precarity cast deep shadows of anxiety, depression, rage, and hopelessness.

Regardless of the extent of our assets, we are all affected by late capitalism's continuing wars, periods of collapse, and sense of impending implosion and environmental apocalypse; its substitution of individualism for interdependence, of entertainment for public dialogue; of militarized police suppression for attempts to dream us beyond the centrifuging process of capitalism that separates those who profit from it from "those who work for it but are systematically excluded by it" (Vallega, 2014, p. 63).

As I reviewed Hillman's writings, I noticed he was slow to write about capitalism. While consistently vocal about the harms of Christianity, he offered a much more fragmentary approach to capitalism, very rarely directly confronting it, trying to see through it, or attempting to adumbrate its archetypal dominants, as he did so brilliantly with other aspects of culture. Instead, he was tracking our ignorance of beauty, urging us to emerge from our anaesthetizing shells to respond to the world around us: to toasters, chairs, buildings, office cubicles, to Zen gardens.

His pointing to the problem of capitalism but not grappling with is a common problem in psychology. There is a pervasive naturalization of the given socioeconomic context and a failure to interrogate its effects on psychological and community life. When Hillman turned to "Soul and Money" in 1982, he was primarily concerned with looking at money archetypally. He did not want to engage in a Christian depreciation of money, to avoid or to flee from it. He held it as "a third thing" between "only spirit and only the world," thus a part of soulful and psychic reality. He proposed, "There is more soul to be found where money problems are most extreme, not in poverty but in luxury, miserly greed, covetousness, and the joy of usury. . ." (2006, p. 364). His essay does not scale up to the psychology of economic systems, beyond noting the co-arising of Protestantism and capitalism. He restricts his analysis to the individual and the dyad of therapy.

Hillman notes the words that bear double meanings for both love and money: "bond, yield, safe, credit, duty, interest, share, and debt." Interestingly, seventeen years later, he makes a stronger set of claims, that even words have been taken over by the "bankers, brokers, and speculators": "trust, interest, growth, goods, develop, security, bond, share, insure, yield, loss, demand, appreciation, industry," and even "welfare" (2006, p. 381). Gone is the medieval understanding of profit as profit for the soul (Fromm, 1976) and of welfare as "happiness, good health, or fortune" (2006, p. 381). In 1997, he points to our system as an oligarchy.

Late in his life the two separate streams of Hillman's attention to beauty and his gathering concern for justice began to flow together and provide us with a point of departure for the work that is needed ahead. Edward Casey (2013) points out that in Hillman's (2008) last book, *Aphrodite's Justice*, Hillman unequivocally links justice and beauty, speaking of beauty's "power (*peitho*) to move the heart toward both love and justice" (p. 40). Casey takes us to what he calls the "heart of the matter" in Hillman's work on justice and beauty:

. . . if beauty is conceived as the fitting and the suitable, its alliance with justice becomes much more accessible. This is what is expressed in the common English phrase 'poetic justice,' which signifies that there is a certain felicity in the working of justice. In this same spirit, the very concept of *kosmos* in the original sense of this word alludes to the marriage of beauty and order: as Hillman avers, *kosmos* 'connotes both aesthetic and ethical order, both adornment and decency.' If the cosmos is aphroditic—if it is beautiful in its appearances —this is only because it is composed of judicious orderings, ways of being just. In this vision, "the walls between the ethical and the aesthetic dissolve." (Casey, in Selig & Ghorayeb, 2014, p. 52)

In his late essay "Justice, Beauty, and Destiny as Foundations for an Ecological Psychology," Hillman (2000) poses what he considers "the most important question for psychology today": "What role has the discipline of psychology in the widest sense played in the progress of this hastening deterioration, and what part might it play in slowing the progress, or better, altering its course?" (p. 210). I offer that part of the answer to these questions is to become clear about psychology's collusion with capitalism, and then—once extricated—to use psychology to understand and support needed alternatives at all levels of scale.

In "Some Costs of American Corporate Capitalism: A Psychological Analysis of Value and Goal Conflicts," Kasser, Cohn, Kanner and Ryan (2007) show how seldom capitalism is presented as a theme in psychological research and journals. They throw into relief the contradiction between capitalism's values (self-interest, strong desire for financial success, interpersonal styles based in competition, [and] high levels of personal consumption), and those that psychologists have come to understand promote psychological and community well being. The former conflict with and undermine pursuits long thought by psychologists to be essential to individual and collective well being (i.e., helping the world be a better place; having committed, intimate relationships; and feeling worthy and autonomous). Kasser et al. underline the false assumption that there is a positive relationship between increased wealth and enhanced happiness. Research is clear that once basic needs and security are met, additional wealth does not increase a sense of happiness in one's life. If human propensities for community, affiliation, benevolence, self-worth, and autonomy are undermined by a system of economic arrangements, then those committed to the promotion of psychological health need to clarify this contradiction and lend their weight to co-creating alternatives.[2]

But psychology, rather than setting itself at odds with large-scale corporate capitalism that has no triple bottom line that includes environmental and social costs and benefits, has adapted its own theories and methods to support this system. This has entailed the embrace of falsely universalized ethnocentric and individualistically oriented psychodiagnostics that strip the wider sociocultural context from the suffering person, and the wholesale adoption of short-term cognitive behavioral approaches and psychopharmaceutical treatments that are considered most cost-effective.

Archetypal psychology and Hillman himself cannot escape this critique. But if we gather together the later fragments relevant to capitalism in Hillman's work, we have a vantage point from which we can begin to see through capitalism. This is not easy. Fredric Jameson, a critic of late capitalism, said "Someone once said that it is easier to imagine the end of the world than to imagine the end of capitalism." Philosopher Timothy Morton (2013) calls capitalism a "hyperobject"—so huge that we cannot begin to get an effective purchase on it, much less to reduce its baneful effects on human beings. But this is exactly what we must do.

In "Ten Core Ideas of Environmentalism," Hillman in 2000 defines "responsive environmentalism" as a movement "from the anesthesia of passive acceptance" to responsiveness formed from the "congenital responses of an intelligent organism in a shared world" (2006, p. 332). He argues that it is our apathy and laissez-faire acceptance that are our enemies, more so than "developers, profiteers, polluters, and grandiose consumers" (p. 333). "The urge to engage, the sense of responsibility arising spontaneously in protest to ugliness, carelessness and waste, and in defense of beauty and value, shows that an aesthetic response is also political action" (p. 333). Our failure to grasp that we belong to the larger whole "drive[s our] acquisitive consumption" (p. 333).

In 1997 Hillman makes an important turn from toasters and chairs to our turning from "the homeless bag lady, the child who sleeps in a cardboard carton, the disheveled vet," saying it is "those we turn from looking at, looking into the eyes of . . . where the reforms of all abstract figurings of welfare truly must take their start" (2006, p. 382). He warns us not to take capitalist free-market economy as a science, or as a "progressively developing system, . . . or our American Dream" (p. 384). Our economy is also, he says, "a morality, a psychology, and even a monotheistic belief that converts all values into one bottom line."[3] He urges us to reflect on the increasing inequalities and sufferings it generates, particularly for children and the unemployed. He reminds us that the high business world is a crimogenic arena, ripe for corporate deviance. In 2001 in "The Virtues of Caution," Hillman connects his longstanding interest in the aesthetic response to politics: "Our noses too, and our eyes and ears, are political instruments, protesters. An aesthetic response is a political action" (in Leaver, 2006, p. 354).

"The communal sense of justice leads to the shifting of intent from protection of private goods to the promotion of the common good, where 'common good' extends beyond the only or predominantly human" (2006, p. 336). Our path to the common good requires our waking up and engaging in "the long-term vision of the common good." We need, Hillman says, to develop a felt sense of belonging to the complex weave of relationships in which we are embedded.

At the end of his essay on welfare, Hillman turns to the elders amongst us and says that if we are true in our desire to promote welfare, the welfare of the whole, then we must face our own avarice, and the consequent sufferings of the increasing poor, especially children.

> Let us not become an airbag nation. Insurance ridden, pension-planned, medicated, anaesthetized, with a self-centered, single-issue pressure group called AARP, an association of the retired! Retirement? Let them put us on an ice floe and shove us out to sea the day we are no longer valuable, but until then we have still much to give back. Have we not the task of elders? . . . There must be grandiosity in our eyes, in our service to that society in the freedom of an enterprising spirit whose pursuit of happiness shows in each act of generosity, with malice towards none and charity for all. (p. 388)

I appreciate the call to elders to face into the destruction wrought by our complicity with the abuses of capitalism. But we cannot leave capitalism to the end of the lives of the affluent, when all gains have been made, and financial security is won. Occupy Wall Street has shown us that at the other end of the life span, the young, who are not yet economically "invested," too many of whom are shut out of any prospect of catching "a rising tide of economic well-being," are busy seeing through the ravages of capitalism, and have set themselves to investing in alternatives. At the edges of capitalism is an astonishing multiplicity of experiments and commitments to recreate the Commons and to commit not to individual economic superiority but to the common shared good: ecovillages, alternative currencies, burgeoning urban gardens, arts projects, permaculture neighborhoods, cooperatives, democratically organized workplaces, participatory budgeting in organizations and even cities. It is here where psyche is graced by gathering vision, and even by some measure of joyfulness and hope in the face of the clouds over earthly existence as we know it. Here at the margins, where depth psychology is supposed to be living its life, outside of therapy and reimbursements, millions of people are putting into place alternatives that could be scaled up as capitalism as we know it—dependent on unlimited resources and growth—lurches destructively towards its final end. Between the young and the old are the rest, entangled at every turn in the invasive virus of capitalism: our job, home, car, insurances, pension, lawyers' fees—or lack of all or most of these—preoccupy us. If we are practicing psychologists every billable hour is entangled with corporate insurance and its definitions of illness and treatment, proscribed diagnostic codes and procedures. Here too is where the courage is needed to bear the contradiction between the aim of our vocation as psychotherapists—care for the soul—and the predatory economic system we work within and all too often work for.

To contribute to the reclaiming and regeneration of the "Commons," our psychologies, including archetypal psychology, need to examine their conscious and unconscious relationship to capitalism, and orient toward a set of critical understandings that can address the deformations and destructions caused by late capitalism. In addition to accompanying those caught in the whirlpools caused by the wake of capitalism, we must also lean into the work of helping to open up and sustain psychic and social space where alternatives can be risked and strengthened, and where the streams of beauty and justice can flow together. It is here that what James called "the thought of the heart" can flourish.

. . . if beauty is conceived as the fitting and the suitable,

its alliance with justice becomes much more accessible.

—Edward Casey

Someone once said that it is easier to imagine the end

of the world than to imagine the end of capitalism.

— Fredric Jameson

NOTES

[1] The enclosure of the Commons that began in 1604 in England expelled families from lands held jointly for the common good. The land was then increasingly owned privately for individual profit.

[2] See Kasser et al. (2007). The emphases in American corporate capitalism tend to oppose, undermine, de-emphasize, and "crowd out" goals and values for caring about the broader world, cultivating close interpersonal relationships, and, especially among poorer individuals, feeling worthy and free; notably, such aims are typically associated with psychological well-being, optimal performance, social cohesion, and ecological sustainability (p. 3).

[3] Hillman asks us to "shift our focus from self-help psychology...to what in the economic system makes so many of us feel we are helpless" (2006, p. 386). "[W]elfare reform begins with harnessing and bridling the runaway nightmare called free-market capitalism" (p. 387).

PART III:

POLITICS OF BEAUTY

Klaus Ottmann is the publisher and editor-in-chief of Spring Publications, Inc., and Deputy Director for Curatorial and Academic Affairs at The Phillips Collection in Washington, D.C. At Spring he has been instrumental in publishing the *Uniform Edition of the Writings of James Hillman* (2004 -). His books include *Yves Klein by Himself: His Life and Thought* (2010), *The Genius Decision: The Extraordinary and the Postmodern Condition* (2004), and *The Essential Mark Rothko* (2003). He translated and published the complete writings of Yves Klein (*Overcoming the Problematics of Art: The Writings of Yves Klein*), Gershom Scholem's *Alchemy and Kabbalah*, and F. W. J. Schelling's *Philosophy and Religion*.

KLAUS OTTMANN

No Ethics Without Aesthetics

IN CHAPTER 14 of *City & Soul*, on "Aesthetics and Politics," James Hillman declares that something important is missing from the political discourse, namely the psychological dimension: "Something psychological is missing" (2006, p. 147).

To correct for this deficiency, Hillman proposes an "aesthetic response" that would bring politics and therapy together—a "psychological activism."

We all know the ethical response: "Injustice, oppression, corruption, we see it and react against it" (p. 147). We use the word "unfair" when we discuss the social and political conditions of workers, women, or minorities. But do we ever speak of the "ugliness" of their conditions?

> Do we ever protest and go on strike because of the insulting, repulsive, and just plain ugly places of our work? Of our malls and strips? Of hospital buildings and government decor? Of the materials we handle, the lights we submit to, the "workstations" we are confined within, the lecture halls that we must endure? (p. 147)

Hillman argues that we are aesthetically oppressed, and this aesthetic oppression "affect[s] our bodily feeling, our emotional well-being":

> We deny our aesthetic responses by closing down our senses, our perceptions, and we anesthetize ourselves with loud music in the ears, with Advil and Xanax, with sleeping pills and caffeine and Prozac . . . Too much ugliness . . .
>
> By suppression of our aesthetic responses, we leave the world to itself and isolate ourselves from its plight. No amount of relating and community building will restore us to the world, and restore the world, unless we trust our aesthetic responses. (p. 148)

As Hillman reminds us, the aesthetic is not devoid of moral and ethical value. Hillman's text was originally delivered as a talk at the Tikkun Summit for Ethics and Meaning in Washington, D.C., in April 1996, under the title "Can There Be Ethics Without Aesthetics?" The title of his talk echoes Wittgenstein's famous dictum that "ethics and aesthetics are one," found in the conclusive paragraphs of the *Tractatus Logico-Philosophicus*, one of the most extraordinary books written by a philosopher—a book that in the end declares itself, its propositions, as "senseless":

> My propositions are elucidatory in this way: he who understands
> me finally recognizes them as senseless, when he has climbed out
> through them, on them, over them. (He must, so to speak, throw
> away the ladder, after he has climbed up on it.) (1981, *Tractatus*, 6.54)

Arguably the most "moral" work of logic written since Spinoza's *Ethics* (after which it is clearly modeled) and perhaps the first philosophical self-help book, it encourages its readers to know when to abandon language and logic, and instead trust their imagination: "Whereof we cannot speak, we must be silent" (*Tractatus,* 7). Wittgenstein compared his writing to "a mirror in which my reader can see his own thinking with all its deformities so that, helped in this way, he can put it right" (1980, *Culture and Value*, p. 18). Not unlike the American mathematician, philosopher, and logician Charles Sanders Peirce before him, who argued for a "fuzzy" or "magic" logic of abduction, Wittgenstein proposed letting go of logic within logic.

Wittgenstein's sentence "Whereof we cannot speak, we must be silent" is the very last sentence of the *Tractatus* and thus somewhat mirrors the very first sentence ("The world is everything that is the case / Fall [*Die Welt is alles, was der Fall ist*]" [1]), which, using the ambiguous German word *Fall*, points even more strongly at an underlying ethical discourse (by alluding to the original sin and man's subsequent Fall from paradise), at a theological-ethical layer underneath logic. In his later *Lecture on Ethics*, Wittgenstein announced on the outset that his topic is really aesthetics: "I am going to use the term Ethics in a slightly wider sense, in a sense in fact which includes what I believe to be the most essential part of what is generally called Aesthetics" (1993, *Philosophical Occasions*, p. 38). Ethics and aesthetics constitute, for Wittgenstein, the realm of absolute and ineffable truths, expressed in ethical and religious statements. Ethical and religious expressions are in essence "nonsensical." "I see now that these nonsensical expressions were not nonsensical because I had not yet found the correct expressions, but that their nonsensicality was their very essence" (1993, p. 44). In a logic made up exclusively of statements of fact, ethics and religion are deterritorialized, oppressed, and, like beauty, beyond language:

> For all I wanted to do with them was just to go beyond the world and
> that is to say beyond significant language. My whole tendency and, I
> believe, the tendency of all men who ever tried to write or talk Ethics
> or Religion was to run against the boundaries of language. (p. 44)

Wittgenstein first describes this boundary in the concluding chapters of the *Tractatus*: "The sense of the world must lie outside the world." (1981, 6.41). And he concludes: "It is clear that ethics cannot be expressed. Ethics is transcendental. (Ethics and aesthetics are one.)" (6.421).

Wittgenstein's famous dictum has to be read in the context of the philosopher's understanding of philosophy as a *living practice*. Ethics includes an aesthetical component, and vice versa. For Wittgenstein—as for Nietzsche before him—art and morality are closely tied. All aesthetic activity is also ethical, just as philosophy is a practice of life, a *Lebensphilosophie*. Philosophy and art are forms of life: To imagine a language means to imagine a form of life [*Lebensform*]: "The term "language-*game*" is meant to bring into prominence the fact that the *speaking* of language is part of an *activity*, or of a form of life" (1993, *Philosophical Investigations*, 1:21). In a letter to the Austrian publisher Ludwig von Ficker, Wittgenstein wrote that the meaning of his *Tractatus* is "ethical," and that the work consists of two parts—a written and an unwritten one: "My work consists of two parts: what is on hand and everything I did *not* write. And it is precisely this second part that is most important. The Ethical is quasi defined from within by my book" (Qtd. in Frank, *Stil in der Philosophie*, p. 88).

Ultimately, for Wittgenstein, as for Hillman, the riddle of life, the riddle that defines the human condition, is an *ethical-aesthetic riddle*. "The solution to the riddle of life in space and time lies outside space and time," wrote Wittgenstein (1981, *Tractatus*, 6.4312). The riddle does not exist (6.5) because it lies outside the world. This ethical-aesthetical riddle points to the *transcendental* aspect of ethics, which Roland Barthes has referred to as "the responsibility of forms," and which is also the repressed. As Hillman put it, "Ethics not only coopted beauty but repressed it" (2006, p. 151).

Aesthetics does not replace ethics; "it give[s] ethics sensate images that direct our longings toward ideals, a vision to contemplate, and seduce towards it" (p. 152).

Hillman understood that connecting aesthetics with ethics connects us "more profoundly with the cosmos itself":

> How does your own particular aesthetic response connect with the cosmos? To begin with, the Greek word *kosmos* is originally an aesthetic term; it does not mean vast and empty outer space through which sealed-up cosmonauts fly at great cost. It meant the right placement of things, fittingly, becomingly, nicely. *Kosmos* was used especially of women with respect to their embellishments. And this meaning continues in our word "cosmetics," which owing to our disparagement of the aesthetic, we see only as superficial, as in "cosmetic surgery," makeup, false front. Whereas "cosmos" means that all things are on display, show themselves, and are presented to the senses, which respond to them with feelings of like and dislike, approval and disapproval, and with a varied and differentiated judgment of their value. Thus your aesthetic responses are cosmological, not merely personal. They are signs that you are here and

taking part in the entire world order, which is from the beginning set out as a pleasing aesthetic display. The world is first of all an aesthetic phenomenon before it is mathematical, logical, or theological. So the most basic reaction to being in the world is aesthetic. That word, *aisthesis*, goes back to a root that means "I breathe in," like sucking in the breath when struck by beauty or horror. Our aesthetic responses are inherently related to the actual world and to the primary way that we take part in it. To suppress these responses is to cop out of the political, that is, out of the common, shared world.

> My final point is that ethics alone is not enough to make a change in the world. Alone, ethics without aesthetics doesn't hold . . . . beauty evokes *love.* (pp. 153-54)

And from love ensues *care* for the world and the other—a transcendental ethics that is not a modality of essence but rather an ethical imperative, a site of responsibility for others. In transcendental ethics, we are ordered toward the face of the other.

Hillman refers to this ethical-aesthetical state where the good and the beautiful come together to induce personal and societal wellness with the Greek expression, *kalos kagathos*, an expression composed of two adjectives, καλός ("beautiful," "noble") and γαθός ("good," "virtuous"). The French philosopher Emmanuel Levinas (1999) called it "otherwise than being," a state where subjectivity substitutes itself for another: it becomes the other in the same. It is inspired by the other, existing through the other and for the other without losing its original identity.

This "otherwise than being" is evidence of the "soul's active participation in the world," as Hillman writes in a related text ("Aesthetic Response as Political Action," 2006, p. 143). Practiced on a communal level, an aesthetical response evokes a Spinozist love, which "feeds the mind wholly with joy" (*Tractatus de Intellectus Emendatione*, 1.10). It is an *active* joy, one that brings us, as Deleuze has written, "near to action, and to the bliss of action" (1997, *Spinoza: Practical Philosophy*, p. 28), and leads to *ethical care*, and thus to civic well-being:

> An aesthetic perception draws forth our ethical care. First awaken *aisthesis*, breathe in the beauty of the cosmos—the meticulous crawl of an insect, the heave of the frosted earth as winter yields its grip, observe the composite complexity of an ordinary stone, the eddies in the sand as the tide recedes, or hear the early morning bird call. Beauty astounds and pulls the heart's focus toward the object, out of ourselves, out of this human-centered insanity, toward wanting to keep the cosmos there for another spring and another morning. This is the ecological emotion, and it is aesthetic and political at once. (2006, p. 154)

Hillman's psychological activism goes beyond "me" and "you." It goes from individual to *cosmic* imagination. As Nietzsche exclaimed in one of his posthumous fragments:

> To learn step by step to cast off the alleged individual! To discover the errors of the ego! To accept egoism as error! But not to mistake altruism for its opposite! That would only be love for other alleged individuals! No! To go beyond "me" and "you"! To feel cosmically! [*Kosmisch empfinden!*] (1999, KSA, 11 [7])

Hillman takes Wittgenstein's notion that that any creative practice has to contain an ethical component, and a political activism, an aesthetical component, and gives it a *cosmic* dimension, connecting it to a cosmically felt sense of beauty that is based on a shared love of and care for the soul of the city and the world.

Sarah Jackson is a Jungian analyst, visual artist, and writer. In 2014, she presented a lecture on the female hero in contemporary cinema at the biannual meeting of the New York Association of Analytic Psychology (NYAAP). In spring 2015, she presented "Regarding Images: What Visual Art Can Teach Us About Dreams" to the Northampton Jung Society, in Northampton, Massachusetts, as well as lecturing on the female hero at Simon's Rock of Bard College in Great Barrington, Massachusetts. Jackson is a graduate of the C. G. Jung Institute of New York, and holds masters degrees in Archetypal Psychology and Fine Art. She has taught drawing, color theory, and art history, and has exhibited paintings, drawings, and wall sculptures widely. She lives in Great Barrington, Massachusetts, where she has had a private practice for 24 years while raising a daughter. She is now raising a puppy instead, as well as studying tango and dressage.

SARAH JACKSON

"When Beauty Walks a Razor's Edge"
—How Our Sense of Beauty Grows and Changes[1]

1. Introduction

TO BEGIN, I WANT to express my deep appreciation of James Hillman for bringing beauty and aesthetics into psychology. He asked psychotherapy to "reinvent itself as an aesthetic activity" (2006, p. 170), so that beauty could play a role both in psychotherapeutic practice and in life.

I agree with Hillman's statement that "the path to the apprehension of beauty goes by way of ugliness" (p. 203); however, he offered no further explanation or amplification of this process. I am interested in what actually happens when we begin to apprehend beauty via ugliness.

Hillman has shown how the soul naturally pathologizes—his term for "the soul's autonomous ability to create illness, morbidity, disorder, abnormality, and suffering in any aspect of its behavior and to experience and imagine life through this deformed and afflicted perspective" (1976, p. 57). We often recoil from these phenomena of the soul, finding them ugly.

If the soul has this propensity, this "afflicted perspective," what about beauty? I propose that if we stick with pathologized images and tolerate them, we can begin to find beauty there, and our sense of beauty will grow and be expanded in the process. This paper is a brief examination of how visual art can and does teach this.

2. Sticking with the Image

"The ground of love," according to Hillman, is in the "very irremediableness" of the image (2006, p. 137). When we stick with the image—staying with it long enough to suspend judgment and remaining curious enough to begin to really see it, we also gradually begin to love it, and to feel loved by it—even if what arrests us initially seems to have been ugliness.[2]

Hillman quotes Thomas Aquinas, who stated that "beauty arrests motion" (p. 193). Conversely, when we deliberately arrest our motion in order to contemplate an image, the longer we stay still and look, the more we see, and the more beautiful it becomes. I learned something important about this from the art historian Michael Fried, in a lecture course I audited while at college. He told us that we had to "put in our time" in front of paintings, particularly Fernand Leger, who was a great favorite of his. (I did not share his enthusiasm so I disobeyed his orders even though I remembered them. However, while preparing this paper, I looked at some Legers and found quite a bit more in them than I had before.)

In order to want to put in time in front of a work of art, something has to beckon us, then arrest us long enough for the image to begin to "flirt" with us. This idea of flirting comes from another of my teachers, Arnie Mindell, founder of Process Oriented Psychology. An exercise he gave us during a workshop consisted of looking around the room with partially closed eyes, noticing the room itself and the objects in it, inviting our awareness to register something that seemed to be beckoning or signaling to us. This sense of attraction to, and from, an inanimate object is what Mindell calls a "flirt."

When we spend time with an image, we literally begin to see and feel it more deeply. There is a physiological underpinning to this as well: the rods and cones in our eyes actually take time to become fully activated. The longer we look, the more we see.

Our individual sense of taste and aesthetics needs to be refreshed and encouraged, as well as challenged, by being subjected to an occasional stretching process. That way, our sense of beauty can grow; otherwise, it remains static and can become ossified.

The job of art is to offer that experience, that stretch, though of course not all art will. We have to find the particular images that perplex and vex us while at the same time flirting with us: offering us just enough to keep us standing there. In this way, art very much resembles dreams, which constantly challenge our habitual points of view and ego positions.

Twentieth and twenty-first century artists have also shown us how modern urban and industrial environments can serve both as raw material and inspiration for art. The best of this artwork continues to expand our aesthetics, helping us to feel love for images and find beauty in places where we might not otherwise have seen it. From the I-beams, channel irons, winches, and vices of the 1950s, which Mark di Suvero, Tony Smith, and others made into sculpture, to Joseph Beuys' hunks of beef tallow, slabs of lead, and rolls of felt, and Eva Hesse's experiments with fiberglass, artists have transformed our ways of looking at industrial materials and urban landscapes and cityscapes.

3. The Pathologized Image: Philip Guston

I felt my own sense of beauty stretching and growing in the course of one afternoon while looking at the paintings of Philip Guston. This occurred a little over ten years ago at a major retrospective of his work at the Metropolitan Museum of Art.[3] Guston had been an abstract painter, but in the late 1960s he began to allow recognizable images to emerge, and these morphed into strange figures and objects. I had always found these paintings rather repellant, even though I recognized their originality as well as their sometimes extreme idiosyncrasies. I saw how influential his work was—I knew painters who continued to imitate him in one way or another—but I still felt like I was biting down on nails when I looked at his later paintings.

Figure 9.1. *San Clemente* by Philip Guston (1975).
Reprinted with permission of the McKee Gallery, New York.

I went to the museum with my eleven-year-old daughter, who under-standably found the paintings both puzzling and disturbing. As we looked at them and talked about them, I found myself seeing them differently, particularly a painting of Nixon entitled *San Clemente* (fig. 9.1). As I began explaining to my daughter what had happened to that unfortunate president, I realized how pow-erfully this painting expressed the disgust, shame, and anger that so many of us felt, both while Nixon was in office and during his forced resignation. The power of Guston's weird, quirky images began to sink in. By the time we were ready to leave, I realized that I felt energized and excited; delight had arrived unan-nounced. I felt different; something in me had changed and the paintings were what had changed me.

I began to love those paintings that day, and I have loved them ever since, but it is not an easy love. It is like having a crabby old uncle who smokes cigars and always smells a little bit bad, who goes to prize fights and hangs out with derelicts, reads philosophy and watches cartoons, asks questions that make you think and says things that make you laugh.

4. How Does Ugliness Shift from Being Frightful to Being Fruitful?

So, I want to try to describe in a bit more detail the transition from ugliness to beauty. First the image seems repellant, yet somehow arrests you. Something has to beckon from within the experience of repulsion. For me with Guston, it is the way the paint is put on, the aliveness of the surface and the edges where colors meet.

This is where individual sensibility has to be allowed and understood, and where personality, and perhaps typology, enters in. Being a feeling type, I respond more to expressive painting, whereas a thinking type might gravitate toward art that is more intellectually driven.

Here are a few rules of thumb. Do not expect to understand what you are looking at. In fact, trust your experience of not knowing and not understanding; it's just as vital with art as with dreams. Trust your discomfort: when your sense of beauty is growing and expanding, it's going to feel uncomfortable because the image is challenging and perplexing. It may not taste good right away—pleasure comes later.

If you think it would look good over a sofa, it's probably not an image that will cause your sense of beauty to grow.[4]

Stop, allow yourself to be arrested, yet try to stay receptive and open. Follow Hillman's advice to the letter: take an interest in an image as it is, be curious about its nature, stay with it longer, " . . . [let it] show itself further, let it speak, enact, grow its wings" (2006, p.137). Hillman continues to remind us that "unless the heart is opened," the aesthetic response has not been stirred. "Let the heart be stirred" (p. 186).

When we take the time to really look at and stick with pathologized images, particularly art that beckons us, our sense of beauty will grow, things will begin ". . . to flame out, like shining from shook foil" (Hopkins, 1877), and our hearts will be expanded in the process.

NOTES

[1] A line from Bob Dylan's 1975 song "Shelter From the Storm."

[2] Hillman derived the phrase "sticking with the image" from Jung's statement that "in order to understand the dream's meaning, I must stick as close as possible to the dream images" (1984, CW 16, para. 320).

[3] The retrospective took place 27 October 2003 through 4 January 2004 and included more than 75 paintings and drawings from 1930 to 1980, the year of Philip Guston's death.

[4] This rule of thumb was put forth by my friend, the artist Peter Acheson.

I felt different; something in me had changed

and the paintings were what had changed me.

—Sarah Jackson

...the path to the apprehension of beauty goes
by way of ugliness.

—James Hillman

Dennis Patrick Slattery, Ph.D., is Core Faculty, Mythological Studies at Pacifica Graduate Institute. He has been teaching for 43 years. He is the author, co-author, editor, or co-editor of 20 volumes, including five volumes of poetry. His recent works are *Day-to-Day Dante: Exploring Personal Myth Through The Divine Comedy* and *Riting Myth, Mythic Writing: Plotting Your Personal Story.* Forthcoming is a collection of essays on psyche and poetics, *Creases in Culture: Essays Toward a Poetics of Depth.*

The Aesthetics of the City: Moments of Arrest

BOOKS CAN SURPRISE US by how often they find a way into our literary and personal lives. Henry A. Giroux's *The Violence of Organized Forgetting: Thinking Beyond America's Disimagination Machine* (2014) is first of all a disturbing book, but it is also a complement to James Hillman's perspectives on politics and aesthetics. Giroux writes early on of the dissolution of democracy as an ideal in American life since the 1970s; he then offers this conclusion:

> Schools, libraries, the airwaves, public parks and plazas, and other manifestations of the public sphere have been under siege, viewed as disadvantageous to a market-driven society that considers noncommercial imagination, critical thought, dialogue, and civic engagement a threat to its hierarchy of authoritarian operating systems, ideologies, and structures of power, domination, and control. (p. 32)

Giroux's commentary on those elements of society that some believe disrupt commerce is akin to Hillman's understanding of *aesthesis* in *City & Soul* as a critical constituent in a culture to encourage its flourishing:

> The word for perception or sensation in Greek was *aesthesis*, which means at root a breathing in or taking in of the world, the gasp, "aha," the "uh" of the breath in wonder, shock, amazement, an aesthetic response to the image (*eidolon*) presented. In ancient Greek physiology and in biblical psychology the heart was the organ of sensation: it was also the place of imagination. (2006, p. 36)

Several of Hillman's most insightful writings on aesthetics and its complicity with ethics for the health of a culture are gathered in *City & Soul* and provide the core material for this essay. In the current cultural paralysis that emphasizes one's economic state of being, he insists that we must have the courage to stand up for our "aesthetic sense" as an antibody to the "pall of numbing conformity [which] deadens our language, our food, our work-places and city streets" (p. 145). When an individual or an entire population suppresses the aesthetic response, "we leave the world to itself and isolate ourselves from its plight" (p. 149). World rebuilding cannot occur without a major virtue that aesthetics promotes and undergirds: Trust. To lose trust is to deny or reject the aesthetic response; further, we lose trust in the animal sense of things, the way and intensity things, people, and objects in the world attract or repel us. Blunting such a crucial faculty of culture seems a major intention of the intensifying and relentless engineering taking place today to fashion a new myth, one which denies critical and aesthetic responses as well as the ability to discern and to exercise a sense of taste.

Hillman discerned such a societal reduction of life's qualities to economics and to a throwaway impulse well before many of us even noticed it as a green blip on the screen. He wrote his way toward heading it off before the debacle of disposability that laces today's consumer culture dug into the soul's soil. Noticing, seeing clearly, paying attention to the details and to the particularities of things, objects, ideas, and images italicize for him an aesthetic presence as well as stimulate a form of alertness that weds once more ethics to aesthetics. Separated, as they are today, both easily fall into oblivion or are maimed into disuse. United they command; divorced they cripple:

> I'm suggesting that all our ethical concerns for justice and fairness, for decency, require as well an aesthetic vision, such as images of the biblical and classical ideals of Jerusalem, the city on the hill, Zion, the restoration of the Temple, the image of Athens and its Acropolis, the cities of the Renaissance like Florence and Venice, images of Paradise, of Eden. (2006, p. 152)

Moreover, coupled with aesthetics and ethics is language itself in both its eloquent and infirm conditions. Words themselves carry soul; it is part of Hillman's frequent mantra: to develop a poetic basis of mind, which is to speak such a poiesis in a language that enjoys and employs health, stamina, and freshets of phrase. One might look then to the health of language in its freedom from clichéd expressions, worn-out locutions, conventional knee-jerk sentences, soundbytes, and unconscious use of anemic metaphors to diagnose the soul illness of an individual, a city, and a civilization. It is one measure to learn to observe; it is quite another to find renewed language, free from group-speak, up-talk, upchuck, and the dead mutton of exhausted words that comprise another form of the malady of "psychic numbing," a term Hillman borrows from the cultural historian Robert J. Lifton.

In chapter fifteen, "Natural Beauty without Nature," Hillman argues against separating beauty from the quotidian order of things: buildings, fence posts, drinking fountains, fish aquariums, graffiti, and pop music. Placing beauty in nature or in a painting misses the point of aesthetics that underlies it. He therefore unfurls a series of proposals to help with "disentangling the need for beauty from the need for nature" so to cease splitting "the natural from the urban" (2006, p. 166). We can recognize Hillman's deliteralizing impulse when his imagination deconstructs what we have accepted as formal properties of places like "nature" and "wilderness." By contrast, he envisions beauty occupying an ideal wilderness, as one example among many; this way of imagining "can be fostered by the attitude of walking the world without injury to it, leaving no trace, no leftover actions to be dealt with by others, giving priority to the physical thing over the subjective will" (p. 170). We sense here an enactment of beauty, a nascent sense of ethics and political action as ecological awareness all at once. Also, and not least present, is an attitude of humility, of humus, of humane treatment of the particulars to allow them the dignity to flourish in the soil of soul. I find most fascinating here and elsewhere his process of seeing down, into, and through as a reclamation of not just an earlier economy but also an earlier mythic sensibility toward all things. Ecology then assumes the garment of psychological aesthetics.

An additional arena of beauty's absence, and for which it does a disservice to the practice, is his discussion of therapy: "and the aesthetic plays no role whatsoever in therapeutic practice, in developmental theory, in transference" (p. 174), nor in successful or failed therapy or when it terminates. His lament drills deeper to embrace the world's current condition, highlighted by a chronic forgetfulness that beauty attends the daily particulars in innumerable ways we no longer notice, witness, or cultivate. Beauty performs benevolent service as mucilage of the soul that holds the world together in a particularly organized way. Ignoring or debasing such a quality or attitude under the mistaken idea that it really does not matter affects the very way we see matter and make certain elements in our personal lives matter, what Hillman will call the world's "inherent radiance," which "lights up more translucently, more intensively within certain events" (p. 178).

The mythical figure of Aphrodite carries the impulse of beauty in Hillman's mythical method; where her mythic presence informs an individual and a culture she is present as "a sense of the world," as a form of divine enhancement (p. 179). She brings the world into a *kosmos*, which he translates as "fitting order, appropriate, right arrangement, so that attention to particulars takes precedence over universals" (p. 180). Aphrodite's influence grounds us in the beauty of concrete things, making even ideas into matter.

Finally, Hillman's brilliance is powerfully present when he describes the benefits of one of the most marginal forms of fear in our society, street gangs, resuscitating not just beauty but its relation to an ethic, a code, a form of behaving that while not accepted by a larger public, works very effectively within the backdrop of gang membership and the streets. "Appreciate the display: the hairstyles, tattoos and piercings, the attention to dress, the value of shoes, of jackets, the rapid transit of fashions. Listen to the beat in the language; watch the dance in the walk, the formalities of greetings, the words that indicate an eye for style, elegance, display. Show for its own sake" (p. 198).

Notice here Hillman's own *aesthesis*: Aphrodite in the specific details, a scent of Helen's beauty in particularities, the poetics of the rhythm of his language. The end-stopped fragment—"show for its own sake." His poetic genius, his mytho-poetic couplings, links the mythology of gangs to their revisioning and reviving aesthetics for the entire culture. Their own brand of poiesis is mirrored in Hillman's language describing it. Go to the margins to see the clear outline of things; see the clear reflection in what is rejected. Reflection in remembrance—seeing from a different window, through a different lens, hearing with different ears, being attuned to the beat of hip-hop, indigenous language, identity through style, fashion, creation, flipping a mass-produced Chevy or Nissan Altima into a stylized low-rider painted with a brilliant lacquer that makes the eyes tear up; displaying a gang's cryptic logo—it all glistens under the lamp of genius.

In ancient Greek physiology and in biblical psychology

the heart was the organ of sensation:

it was also the place of imagination.

—James Hillman

I'm suggesting that all our ethical concerns

for justice and fairness,

for decency,

require as well an aesthetic vision...

—James Hillman

Matthew Green, Ph.D., is Director of Academic and Social Programs for Cuesta Community College and lead facilitator of the Central Coast Jung Society in San Luis Obispo. For 15 years, he served as an academic director in college study abroad programs, which was the context for investigating the concept and practice of teaching poetic awareness. He presents this experience in a chapter of the book *Reimagining Education: Essays on Reviving the Soul of Learning,* edited by Dennis Slattery and Jennifer Selig, and more fully in his dissertation entitled, *Poetic Awareness: Imagination and Soul in Education.* He has taught and led seminars on depth psychology and culture, and in March 2012, he was one of the speakers at the Hillman Memorial held at Pacifica Graduate Institute.

Teaching Poetic Awareness

IN VOLUME TWO of the *Uniform Edition*, in a chapter entitled simply "City," James Hillman makes this observation: "The city asks for discovery, for fresh perception, not for new planning; the secret city, the momentary eternal city that springs from imagination and surprises the heart. We may catch it in a glance through a doorway, reflected in a puddle, heard in the closing of a heavy door" (2006, p. 18). In this brief passage, Hillman captures the essence of the project of study abroad that I discuss in this essay.

For fifteen years I worked as a director and teacher of college study abroad, primarily in the city of Toulouse in the southwest of France. Students would come to France for fifteen weeks to learn the language and about the culture through direct encounters with the French and their world. With this backdrop of learning about France, what I was striving to accomplish, to facilitate in terms of the students' learning and experience, had to do with *poetic awareness*; it was an education in perception, imagination, and surprises of the heart.

The program asked the students to engage the world around them and to learn from that engagement. The students were sent not to the library but to cafés and department stores, historic sites and community events, flea markets and wherever the students' hearts and curiosity led them. They went into the streets; they went into the city.

I recognize that the program was asking a lot of the students; it disrupted both the "what" and the "how" of the learning they were used to. The "what" was no longer simply the facts about France on a homework assignment or exam, asking the number of Renault cars built in a year, for example, or the percentage of energy that comes from nuclear power. The "what" was now both France and *themselves*, their capacity to see, to notice, and respond with the heart to the world of their encounters. And the "what" of France was not the predictable face of the culture they expected, but the face *they* discovered in their encounters with the city.

The "how" of this approach asked the students to notice and engage aspects of life, of community, that, for many, had never landed on their radar, or fallen within their corridor of experience, of familiarity and comfort. But the city, especially a grand city like Paris or Toulouse was and is an ideal context for awakening the poetic mind, even more to a foreigner.

I understood that each of the students' encounters was an invitation to a relationship—with the stories and qualities inherent in the event, in the landscape of the city. I knew that the students' encounters held unfathomable potential of experience. Yet so often this potential remained dormant or was rejected and passed them by. I eventually came to see that the more the inner life or the imaginational participation of the student was involved in the encounter, the more the qualities, the interiority, the soul of the event came alive to the student.

The activities and assignments during the semester invited the students to shift their preoccupation from themselves and learn to pay attention, register and interiorize features and qualities around them. For the students, it was about discovering France. For me, France was a pretext. The core of the learning had to do with awakening the students' aesthetic response and allowing the qualities of the city to unfold and take shape in them, as images, and move them to respond, engage and into action. Initially I was disappointed and frustrated by how passive and disengaged students could be regarding their surroundings and their encounters. Their capacity and even inclination to notice and have an aesthetic response in dialogue with the world was often limited. This limitation, I thought, compromised and even sabotaged their learning and experience of France. It didn't take long, however, for me to appreciate that the learning was actually about the aesthetic response and not about France.

For most students this learning was a slow, painstaking, uncomfortable, and prickly process. It often took students the entire semester to accept, finally to move into the conditions of this mode of learning, this mode of knowing. Fortunately, the group arrived in Paris initially and would stay for five days. Paris was infallibly so enchanting that the students were predisposed at the outset to be engaged, to be stirred. A critical feature of teaching poetic awareness is taking advantage of the natural lures of the environment that jump start the imaginative participation of the students.

On the first full day of the program the students plunged into the city. Each was given the name of a different Paris metro station and four or five words that had some association with the surrounding area. The students left for the day and then returned and related what they had learned about the words, and the site—the people and activities. The adventures and discoveries the students shared were charged with wonder, enchantment, and elation, and sometimes with disappointment, shock, and disgust. The discussion that ensued set the stage for a semester of reflection, of reconsidering and reimagining. Imagine a student reporting back incensed that the area surrounding her metro station was boring and unfriendly, and that this inhospitality kept her from learning about her words or really discovering any details about the area. While acknowledging that the student's response may indeed reflect qualities of the place, in the group discussion she would likely be invited to consider that her impression and learning experience might also stem from her particular involvement. She would hear other students describe a different face of Paris and a different approach to engagement. Or imagine a student returning delighted by how fun the adventure was as he describes a day of encounters where all the attention and focus was on him and little or none was on the world he intended to discover.

I share this detail of the first activity to highlight the fact that the teaching and learning did not dwell in the abstractions of theories and concepts, but in the lived experiences, emotions, and reactions of the students. The teaching started with *where* the students were, with *who* they were. In this activity, the students were asked to suspend their subjective view, their preconceived and self-referential notions and reactions, and instead imagine a dialogue with the features and qualities of the landscape itself, paying attention to the images and reactions that emerge from direct observation of what was there and what was going on rather than filtered through and prompted by habit and expectation. *It was so much easier said than done.* It often took doing it with them or alongside them to help them see what possibilities were there to notice and respond to.

On day three of the program the group would stroll, attentive and in silence, through the historic Marais District, attend mass at Notre Dame, and then, in a café on Isle St Louis, imagine the stories these places tell of themselves and reflect on the proposition Lawrence Durrell (1960) makes in his article "Landscape and Character" that there is a spirit of place, an invisible constant, in each landscape that a traveler can get a sense of with ten minutes of quiet inner identification. "It is there," writes Durrell, "if you just close your eyes and breathe softly through your nose; you will hear the whispered message, for all landscapes ask the same question in the same whisper: 'I am watching you—are you watching yourself in me?'" (p. 158).

In this exercise, repeated in different forms and configurations throughout the semester, the students were encouraged to heed Durrell and remain silent, what Hillman (2006) suggests the soul requires to allow space for imagining, for images to draw and hold our attention and concentrate our thoughts and feelings, suspending action (p. 82). In this silence, the attention extends outward to the features of the encounter and inward to images and aesthetic responses.

In Toulouse and for the remainder of the semester, the students would attempt to hold this perspective as they described the city from the sixth floor of Nouvelles Galleries department store, explored the Renaissance architecture of the grand townhouses that define the city, spent time at a monastery, participated in a rap sharing and potluck at a community center, or strolled on a Sunday afternoon along the Garonne River. These experiences moved the students to connect with and recognize these contexts as mattering on their own terms, for their own sake.

A fundamental challenge of the program was teaching students who had become anesthetized—fundamentally bored—by an approach to learning that had generally treated them as "consumers and processors of information." Their conception of learning did not readily include experience or learning from their own experience, let alone learning *to* experience. Early on the students would be inclined to say, "Just tell me what I need to know for the test." Teaching poetic awareness involved loosening the grip of identity that held each student.

The first step was for the student to recognize that opening the classroom to the world was legitimate. An often bigger second step for the students was accepting that learning to participate, imaginally, in an animated landscape was a valid undertaking for these studies. And, finally, accepting that who they are, their personality, their identity, was part of the learning equation. This program ultimately shattered their idea of how we do education and what it is for.

The reality of teaching poetic awareness in a study abroad program was that every incremental movement of the students necessitated a relentless presence and structure that compelled them to describe, respond, and react to, and imagine differently the world of their encounters. As the students shifted from imagining themselves as having bought a ticket to a museum to participate in an animated world, the qualities of soul of the city would impress upon them. Encounters with the city pulled them in and down—into reflections of recessed dimensions in nocturnal meeting places, into interior images of a sometimes awkward Sunday dinner with the host family, into the emotional memory of a favorite hangout or a jarring historical site, into images of rivers and bridges, arches and bricks, and into eye-level, face-to-face human interactions in the café-bar Le Brueghel, Place Arnaud Bernard. This experience, this prolonged encounter with the city, was often disruptive and revelatory of their patterns and identities often leading to a breakdown and eventually a breakthrough. It was after the awareness stemming from this breakthrough dawned on them that students would inevitably ask, "Why didn't you tell me this before?"

PART IV:

PLACES OF PRACTICE

Rodney C. Teague, Ph.D., resides outside the town of Notasulga in rural, central Alabama with his wife Erin Leigh; sons Tal and Ches; daughter Emma Ruby; two hobo dogs, Allie and Bo; and until recently, two elderly cats, now buried in a corner of the lot. He was born and reared in central Oklahoma. As a child wandering the ranchland there, he discovered a stone-roofed "dugout" that was tucked into the prairie during land-run days, and which he considers his imaginal first home. For eighteen years preceding his current country-mouse experiment in Notasulga, Teague lived in Atlanta, Dallas, and Pittsburgh (where his two sons were born) while earning a doctoral degree in Clinical Psychology from Duquesne University. While at Duquesne—and previously at the University of Dallas—he studied psychology as a human science from existential, phenomenological, and critical perspectives. He came to psychology initially through literature—through Faulkner, Dostoevsky, and Shakespeare viewed in light of a collective (un)conscious, and he continues to make his way back to and through literature. Mentors at the University of Dallas, the Dallas Institute, and Duquesne University nurtured—and go on nurturing—this trajectory. Currently, his clinical work is with veterans who are diagnosed with mental illness, addictions, and who have had experiences of combat and other trauma. This work connects him to his late grandfathers, both decorated World War II veterans. It also connects him with the vast capacity of the human soul for suffering and resilience. Existential and narrative perspectives inform his work.

RODNEY C. TEAGUE

Going to Town, Being in Town, Leaving Town

I READ THE FIRST chapters of *City & Soul* with a defensive reaction, given our decision six years ago to quit city life and move our family to the country—what we have called our "country-mouse" experiment. I felt that James Hillman was unfairly attacking my lifestyle choice. But I got over it and the resulting reflections have been at least personally fruitful.

Going to Town

The country mouse and city mouse fable has many iterations. Most advance a moral contrary to Hillman's. In fact, it is the position against which he contends: the fantasy that the soul is best off in nature where it can avoid the corrupt sophistication of cities. In Aesop's version, the town mouse visits his country cousin and, unimpressed by the meal he is offered, bids the "rough and ready" cousin to return with him to the city where he can show the bumpkin "how to live." Though Aesop ends with the expected conclusion—that it is better to enjoy a simple life than to live in fear—another, perhaps unintended lesson is embedded in the tale: how can you be satisfied with this bland fare, my boy? The city is where you can *learn how to live*. There's a wink in the moralizing. The hidden salience of the story involves movement, commerce, and intercourse between symbolic lifestyles. So, why do we go to town?

The story goes, in my family, that in the hours immediately preceding his death, my great grandfather declared to his son, my grandfather, "I don't believe I'm gonna be able to make it up onto the wagon for the trip to town today." Great Grandfather passed long after the triumph of the automobile over mule wagon. As for which town he would not visit again, it may have been Altus, in western Oklahoma, or maybe back in his native Arkansas, but either way, you can bet it was small. No world-class city with grand monuments to Mnemosyne, I am certain. Still, I am compelled by his deathbed imagining. I wonder what so captured his longing? It is hard for me to believe he was thinking about selling eggs and butter.

I think of Eudora Welty's old, blind Phoenix picking her careful "worn path" along the Natchez Trace at Christmastime, toward town, the clinic, and soothing medicine awaited by the grandchild at home (1982, p. 142). Despite the urgency of her mission, the journey itself tantalizes her with marble cake, dancing, and dangerous ill-gotten gains in the form of a pilfered nickel. With her medical mission finally accomplished and ten cents to the good, she delights in her imagination of the paper windmill she will purchase and which will astound the child who awaits her return. These longings and delights overwhelm the ostensible, expedient purposes for the trip to town. The images corroborate Hillman's contention that cities do not exist for economic reasons alone.

But for a journey to a town that is "luxury, *per se*," and "pure appetite," we need swifter conveyance. In William Faulkner's final published novel, *The Reivers*, Lucius, Boon, and stowaway Ned lurch toward a Memphis brothel in the Winton Flyer, the first automobile in Jefferson, stolen from Lucius' grandfather. Lucius, an upright, upper-class preadolescent and our narrator, is approached by Boon with the idea that they should steal away to Memphis. He tells us he had no need of such seduction: "There is no crime which a boy of eleven had not envisaged long ago. His only innocence is, he may not yet be old enough to desire the fruits of it, which is not innocence but appetite" (1992, p. 46). The city beckons as the place of appetite even if we do not know the fruit—the object—of our longing. And the city is the place that will teach the boy "how to live." But what shall we do when we get there?

Being in Town

Big cities are multiple cities. Multiplicities of activity, movement, noise, and strains of voices borne in such variety of languages, dialects, discourses, all independent and yet blending into the seemingly "purposeless cacophonies" that philosopher and critic Mikhail Bakhtin called *heteroglossia* (2006). Now admittedly Bakhtin was talking about novels, but Hillman wrote that cities, in their density, complexity and elegance, are novels. They are novel because, in their complexity and heterogeneity, they present us with novel experience, with contrast and contradiction. This is true for the debutante and the uninitiated (fresh from the country, perhaps) experimenting with unknown and pleasurable consumables of all sorts but equally for the city dweller, as the park bench or cafe provides a respite from the day's busyness.

Once in Memphis, Lucius tells us that he fell "pell-mell" into experiences he was not yet ready to receive. It's safe to say he learned a lot about life. But he will be fine, and we'll return to him later.

Hillman celebrates the anything-goes dimensions of city experience; shoulder-to-shoulder luxuries consuming innocents with an appetite for appetite itself. But how shall we evaluate these city experiences? For surely we can get caught, even among all of the possibilities, in a rut. We get stuck in ways of living that diminish and banish the imaginal world: the workaday rat race, anger and violence, unbalanced consumption of all kinds.

I'll suggest that the good experience of novelty in the city is one characterized by fruitful, imaginative learning and the development of an ironic perspective. In his essays on education, collected as *Unbinding Prometheus*,

Dr. Donald Cowan (1988) has written that learning is the essential imaginative activity and the source of human joy. "Give us this day our daily *hunger*" (p. 93). Cowan quotes Gaston Bachelard (then Dr. Don winks to us, referring to Bachelard as an "avid reader of books," p. 93). A-ha! Our appetite, for which we may not know the fruits, has to do with *learning*. We hunger for something new. The first moment of learning beyond apprehension of the image is, for Cowan, the "critical act." This is the part that stands aside, viewing one's thought, image, and work dispassionately. It is the contemplative act. Cowan continues, "The part that distances itself governs one's learning ability, elevating it to the plane of understanding. The fruit of that understanding is what one does in life, one's critical comment on existence" (p. 84). You see, we must be able to do something with the experiences offered to us by the metropolitan buffet, must be able to reflect upon them in some meaningful and useful way. The fruit of our learning may be externalized as artistic expression, even as the human hand is compelled to make its mark against the impersonal wall in Hillman's city. But this "making," as Cowan puts it, may also refer to reforming one's self-understanding. Cowan writes that through this kind of learning a person may "achieve the true form of his life." The mind that is unable to experience, to learn, in this way falls into despair. This is well illustrated in drug addiction, whose hallmark—increasing "tolerance" for the substance of abuse—is evocatively described as "chasing the dragon." The seemingly auspicious initial experience of euphoria, ecstasy, goes undigested while the individual repeats compulsively and destructively his attempts to approximate that first high.

I do not wish to overestimate intellectual understanding. The contemplative 'stepping aside' we're talking about is a matter of perspective taking. In her history of the Fugitive Poets, Dr. Louise Cowan (1972) describes John Crowe Ransom's understanding of (critical and poetic) irony as the most inclusive state of mind, resulting from the confrontation between romantic illusions about life and life's difficult realities. The necessary rejection of illusions, however, is unwilling, and leaves a residue of "music and color" whose fruit is irony and poetry born of the "whole mind," encompassing "both creation and criticism, both poetry and science" (p. 22). Here, as in Donald Cowan's formulation, experience must lead to fruitful change or production. This seasoned ironic perspective yields creative fruit rather than cynicism and despair. I am aware of the irony of advancing the agrarian poet Ransom to support Hillman's work on the city. However, Ransom's insistence on the preeminence of the world outside the mind and his perspective that, despite its fallenness, "the world's body is inexhaustibly interesting" (p. 18), is nothing short of Hillmanian.

The hermeneutic I am suggesting is a movement between experience and reflection and a resulting cultivation of ironic critical perspective. This means infusing attention to the vicissitudes of psyche into individual subjective concerns as well of those of communities.

Exile

There are many ways to leave town. Lucius' departure and return home has a bit of a tail-between-the-legs quality to it. We will return to him momentarily. First I want to address briefly three notions of leave-taking as exile. The "mentally ill," particularly the impoverished mentally ill, are exiles from the city. What we call the "stigma of mental illness" is exile from the city. It is the continually renewed exclusion of persons whose experiences are deemed unworthy of digestion and incorporation into wholeness of communal understanding. Certainly those labeled and diagnosed are participants of a sort, swept-up and imprisoned as they are in diagnostic language and managed systems of "care." These are the throwaway people, those under the bridges and in the shadows of gleaming towers.

Second, a special subset of these folks is trauma-sufferers, in general, and returning combat service members, in particular. Trauma is, by its very nature, experience that we cannot incorporate meaningfully into our experience, our self-story—both at the level of the individual and that of the community. Re-integration of warriors is an ancient problem for the civil city. Our present version of exile for these warriors is particularly cruel, wrapped as it is in yellow ribbons, parades, and well-meaning but empty expressions of thanks. Real reintegration will require large-scale cultivation of ironic imagination through ritual and art that allows us to communally acknowledge the actions and choices that place our citizens outside the walls of our tolerance, our communal culpability for and participation in their experiences and our willingness to welcome them back into our city with a fullness of understanding, compassion, and outrage.

And what of the psychologist? The psychotherapist? His exile? To lift contemporary practice out of the "anesthetized slumber of subjectivism" alone may require expatriation from the community of established professional practice. David Abrams, in *The Spell of the Sensuous* (1996), argues that the therapist, like the shaman, occupies a place on the margins of civilization—on the edge of town—responsible for mediating between human and other-than-human forces. Similarly, Glen Arbery's (2001) exegesis on Seamus Heaney goes further to suggest that the poet, by virtue of the perspective-taking that informs his craft, enacts betrayals on all parties—may be party to none, must be exiled from all community. As poet/critic/perspective-takers, we psychologists are subject to a similar kind of exile.

My friend and colleague recently suffered the loss of a therapy patient to a fatal heroin overdose. Her grieving over her patient was compounded by her sense of the pervading professional stance that had the therapy had been effective, the event would not have occurred. Her patient was one of the souls who could not find a home in the city. My friend looked hard at the practice of psychotherapy and decided that it does not have the tools to help the city or the soul.

So she resigned her position and left the practice. Perhaps we cannot join the troupe of poets, but as critics in our cultivation of perspective, I think we must be prepared to expatriate ourselves from all familiar practice. We can be professional perspective-takers and story-gatherers rather than trying to be personally useful in curing people.

Finally, what learning can we discern in Lucius' adventure? His grandfather and Ned had some canned-sounding "lessons" for him. But Lucius returned home with a revolutionized sense of the world. And as for the fruitfulness? Faulkner ends his novel with the fertile and comic image of an ugly baby born to Boon and the (former) prostitute Everbe, who tells Lucius that he should have known the child would bear his own name—his "progenitor," an ironic product of that trip to town. Perhaps exile may be reimagined as a protracted process of return—movement between experience and reflection with a commitment to soul. A cycle of visitation between country and city cousins.

Cheryl Sanders-Sardello, Ph.D., is co-founder and co-director of The School of Spiritual Psychology, in Benson, North Carolina. Prior to the founding of The School in 1992, she worked as a counselor of mentally handicapped children, and later as an addictions counselor at Parkland Hospital and Southwestern Medical School in Dallas. She is currently writing a book on the healing of the twelve senses in the young and the development of the spiritual senses as we age, with an additional focus on the spiritual psychology of what it means to be in connection with the "so-called dead." She creates healing mandalas in the context of the classes within The School, and is involved in research of all aspects of Spiritual Psychology. She is also the administrative director of The School, coordinating and scheduling its activities, and is a Fellow of the Dallas Institute of Humanities and Culture.

CHERYL SANDERS-SARDELLO

You Have the Right to Remain Silent

HILLMAN GAVE A KEYNOTE address in 1987 in which he speaks of the nature of silence in the context of therapy with children. In this presentation he used the Miranda rights statement to make a point about the interiority of the phenomenon of silence. In his talk he points out that silence, ultimately, is a "right," as in "you have the 'right' to remain silent"—as we all know, the rest of the statement is, "anything you say can and will be used against you in a court of law . . . ," etc. Hillman asserts that we believe that "rights" are the basis of all freedom; that "rights" are inalienable, we come with them; they are not 'given' to us. Most intriguing. The "right" to 'be' silent, or the 'right of silence'?

That the "right" to remain silent, legally the right not to incriminate oneself, where what you say can be used against you, is also true in life in general, for example, in therapeutic situations, at all levels of civic engagement, and academia, politics, and business . . . every arena . . . what we say can and often is "used against us," so that we become circumspect and downright paranoid about speaking. Or, alternately, we spout off our opinions as if they were solid fact and intimidate and abuse others by our inability to remain silent—meanwhile keeping them silent by default. The "right" becomes power, or is considered a weakness.

Hillman gives us the beautiful image of the silence of the animal, the deep soul silence, not hiding or attacking, just dwelling within and of the being; "noticing," he says. The silence that listens, watches, holding still and ready; a silence not as something being done, but rather an "is-ness" of silence, silence as noun, as autonomous in itself. He describes the therapeutic tenets of trust, empathy, security, and support resting in what he feels to be the "noticing" within the animal silence. Transcending interpretation, the "noticing" awakens possibilities of soul connection. Could we live in this kind of "noticing" and nurture more silence back into the everyday world, even the city?

Beyond the therapy room, Hillman describes silence as the wellspring of soul carrying imagination into the world, into the home, the workplace, and the city. As soul expands through experience and knowledge, city grows into what imagination can make of it—into what imagination MAKES in its ever unfolding. The basis of the city becomes the imagined ideal, as given and received, through silence.

The city, if first conceived as theory, as a concept derived from thoughts and formulations, results in a place one would not want to live, a rather cold, hostile, possibly even infantile conglomeration of developments and businesses, full of political posers and the drive for power.

However, when the city becomes the unfolding of an imagined, living place, it comes to be something alive, the kind of place in which one would want to live. Homey. Welcoming. Someplace to come back to always.

How striking that silence holds such potential, such fecundity. Silence as a Being, as an archetype, not much noticed, hardly thought of as bearing the foundations of living, yet ever present and longing for our capacity to open into the silence as mother, silence as maker of life, of imagination of living, of holding every possibility.

You have the right to remain silent.

Silence as the origination of rightfulness . . . something that remains, something that is right. Silence as the depth of psyche's freedom. Beyond political freedom, beyond striving or proof. Silence doesn't need to wave a flag or stand for something else. Silence become sovereign. Autonomous. Perhaps even ascendant.

We have the right to remain silent. When we give up that right, anything we say can and will be used against us.

It is as if the imaginal will not bear being denied the expression of its nature, silence. Silence, the Being, gives the imaginal, ever-expanding story. The story only "told" from the silence. Not the accounting of details that are enumerated from memory. Memory cannot create, only recreate. It has to hear to testify. Silence plants and nurtures, bears and buries.

If the soul gives birth to the city, it emerges from soul longing, born out of silence. We draw forth, imagine into being that which connects . . . arrange and rearrange imaginal connections that are allowed to ripen and transform. Bridges, gardens, cemeteries, azaleas on Preston Road, bluebonnets on Highway 114, great crystals in the plaza, defenseless, but courageously making and holding a place. Longing for a way to reach beauty, we gather the silent beings into our city and are transformed by the presences that collect around them.

Rilke (1910) speaks of being in Paris. Paris seems a hard and even cruel place in its indifference to the individual. He suffers in being alone. His alone-ness is magnified by the innumerable souls he witnesses going about daily life, not noticing him or his loneliness. Then he walks out of his empty room into the night and feels the city surrounding him as a new place. The city has become quieted, softened, has a new face, feels like a qualitatively different place. He feels the longing of the city, its stillness, and its patient silence. Here he finds the city he sought, the one where he came to write. He is transformed by the city's silence.

It's true, isn't it? A city becomes more mysterious, more lonesome deep in the night. It beckons and awaits our attention as it seems to go into its own silence, perhaps to listen to us. But it doesn't "require" night to find the archetypal silence of the city. We feel it in the architecture, the green places, the spaces between one corner and the next—those vast areas where cars vie to be the first through the intersection, when left alone, are acres of silent emptiness, bravely doing their mundane job of keeping order and otherwise being ignored unless we happen to career into another car there . . . then they become an instant memorial.

Museums, galleries, courtrooms, offices, alleys, cemeteries; the silence speaks for the empty space and the soul qualities that fill them. When one walks into the Texas School Book Depository, the silent accumulation of psyche's presence overwhelms us. There, in the empty air, silence holds so much feeling we can feel it crushing into our heart. Or, in the sweet emptiness of the "grassy knoll," would we but listen, the unfolding of the love held in this one tiny spot could carry us for lifetimes through dark and dreary loneliness.

You have the right to remain <u>silent</u>.

You are blessed with the real presence of silence.

Hillman speaks of entering silence without trying to beat a confession out of it; without shutting it down into a fixed but flabby concept that, in trying to mean everything, means nothing. He offers silence as the entry to imagination unfolding, deepening into inspiration, widening into the place of intuition, giving up the known for the opening into possibility. Any possibility. Maybe every possibility? Coming from silence.

In our cities we are sure of the rules. Absolutely positive we know what we are supposed to do in any given moment. We think we are protected by laws. We feel guarded by security and rules of conduct. Even the city knows how to behave to protect itself and to keep growing to prove it is worthy. If the city were the one speaking its troubles to us, the therapist, would we give it its "right to remain silent"? Would we wander its streets at night, when the stillness and the silence allow it to touch us with its longing? In the silence, would the story of the city unfold and deepen in us so acutely, we would know how to nurture it toward the unknown future, rather than "develop" it into banality?

In small, hidden, sometimes surprising secret places, the city's silence lets us know it loves us, too, and keeps longing toward that fountain of imagination that sees clearly what the soul of the city longs for in its silent places of stillness. How do we find these hidden treasures? The search might begin by thinking of the objects in your own home—the ones you cherish that are personally, intimately significant to you beyond their financial value. Those irreplaceable things that were handed down from great grandparents, or that the kids made in kindergarten . . . or that a beloved gave as an apology, or a promise. Those are not just the things we own; they are the holders of silence that draw us into the imaginal, beyond memory, beyond sentimentality . . . the imaginal reality of life, which speaks to us from their silence to our silent heart. And even if we don't think about these things, they are anchors and signposts, holding us, pointing the way, offering support and encouragement through the silence they hold.

The imaginations they inspire. Like places in the city, the silent (note: not neces-sarily "without sound") places of the mysterious imaginal. The places that are ours and "exclusively" possessed by many, unknown to each other. Or the places possessed by all, which are always giving us who we are together.

Soul itself emerges out of the silence children are steeped in. The soul is not a full-blown, total entity at birth, not any more than we are empty slates on which life writes our story. No, we are each born pregnant with soul, but it must steep in the body's presence, in the depth of the infant's silence, and ever vigilant to every nuanced gesture, it emerges in the child as a flowering of being. From the silence.

Children are given the possibility of silence not in their being quiet—or being "quiet"—but in their ability to notice, as the animal notices, from a deep-er place, one not reached when the head becomes filled with knowing about. A place that rises up from the world's just being there—calling—beckoning the soul to come forth. In responding to the world, soul moves into it, dancing and delighting, then comes back into the body with soul images. The imagination quickens into embodied life, and we become human beings.

Everything of the world contributes.

Everything of the world speaks.

(Pointing to the front, north corner of the room, behind the table where books have been laid out for sale, just left of the speaker podium, where, incongruous with the room, a twelve-foot ladder is leaning against the wall.)

Like this silent, self-conscious ladder—not sure why it's been left there—wondering where it really belongs—has been speaking to me all day. I ache to climb it to see what's up there—or to put it somewhere to see if it feels a kind of relief in being released from its corner behind the books, trying to be invisible, while in plain sight to all. It has a right to remain silent—its silence is a right—al-lowing it to remain, even where it seems out of place, not really belonging right now, but nevertheless made to stay in just this place, seen and ignored, invisibly visible, not sure what to do. It bears the soul that ascends to the imaginal city—we are graced by its silent presence, which speaks and does not speak to us, should we but listen to the silent voice being—and let its silence set us free.

...we spout off our opinions as if they were solid fact

and intimidate and abuse others

by our inability to remain silent—meanwhile,

keeping them silent by default.

—Cheryl Sanders-Sardello

As soul expands through experience and knowledge,

city grows into what imagination can make of it...

—Cheryl Sanders-Sardello

Gustavo Barcellos is a Jungian analyst in São Paulo, Brazil, a member of the Associação Junguiana do Brasil (AJB) and the International Association for Analytical Psychology (IAAP). He is the founding member and Editor-in-Chief of *Cadernos Junguianos*, AJB's annual journal since its inception in 2005. He lived in the USA during the 1980s where he finished his M.A. in Clinical Psychology at the New School for Social Research, and studied at the C. G. Jung Foundation, both in New York City. During this period he met James Hillman, with whom he studied and who was later to become his mentor and friend. After coming back to Brazil, he translated several of Hillman's books into Portuguese and is responsible for introducing archetypal psychology to Brazilian students. He is the author of many books and articles in Brazil and abroad in the field of archetypal psychology, imagination and the arts, including a book on the psychology of the brother archetype in 2009, and a book on psyche and image in 2012. He was a contributor to the books *Listening to Latin America—Exploring Cultural Complexes in Brazil, Chile, Colombia, Mexico, Uruguay and Venezuela* and *Psyche and the City: A Soul's Guide to the Modern Metropolis*, edited by Thomas Singer for Spring Journal Books, to which he contributed the chapter on São Paulo, "Harlequin City." He has been professionally involved with Jungian educational and analytical institutes throughout the country and teaches seminars in Jungian and archetypal psychology. He has held a private practice in São Paulo, Brazil since 1985.

GUSTAVO BARCELLOS

South and the Soul

I WANT TO CONCENTRATE upon the idea of "south" and what it means for soul in an attempt at reimagining archetypal psychology's celebrated *southward direction*. In South America, of course, we are inclined to see "south" as still a great metaphor for depth psychology. We cannot escape the feeling of "south," into which we are born. So we need to reflect upon it, that is, create ever-new images. It is a huge cultural complex; in a sense, it is the complex of inferiority, of that which is felt or feels itself as inferior, the underside, even underworld, and we are those *inferiores*. We need to see through this metaphor, and for this we must turn inevitably to *imaginal geography*, or a geography of images, and see the ways in which south is a place for psychological practice.

But, to attempt an archetypal re-vision of the idea of "south" in our psychology, and to give it a deeper significance in our lives, we should not at all go by the way of simple reversion, simply putting north-south upside down, trying for a moment to disturb optics and soul, seeing south as superior. That would be "psychopathic geography": south in the place of north and nothing is really changed in our perspective. Nor would I wish to fall here once again into "those tiresome dilemmas of North and South"—historical geography. No; to be sure, I want to avoid the rhetoric of oppression altogether, so archetypal for the relations between North and South, and so paradigmatic to our continent, the Americas, as James Hillman brilliantly expanded on the one occasion he discussed South America in the article "Culture and the Animal Soul," published in *Spring* in 1998.

Archetypal psychology has brought back this metaphor in particular, "south," to make a major theoretical move. We know this move had to do with the turning of the West-East axis into a North-South axis, which for Jungian psychology meant that we no longer had to go East to go deep. This "south" was meant to be essentially the Mediterranean culture—from Greek myths and religion to Renaissance civilization, philosophy, and modes of living: imaginal sources that brought sensual as well as tragic perspectives to psychology and to psychotherapy.

We know the significance and the power of the south metaphor: it is truly archetypal. Since Freud and the early days of psycho-topographical descriptions, it was *the* place to go when imagining a direction towards the unconscious, towards soul: the vertical direction. To find soul we go downwards: personal memories, childhood, ancient myths, complexes, archetypal reality—all this is imagined to be stored deep down inside, the "south" of ourselves. True character is also imagined to be down inside our acts. And we must not forget this "south" stands as well for the lower part of the body.

The downward direction is, simultaneously with the inward direction, the way the imagination of depth psychology follows: we go "down," we go "south," either in the individual or the culture. Hillman imagined this direction even further in his geographical *poiesis* and said that it, archetypal psychology, "starts in the South" (1985, p. 30). He also wrote, "venturing South is a journey for explorers" (1975, p. 223).

But we know the dark projections that landed below the Equator (the Equator, that abstract line of the spirit that does not really *equate* anything): tropical-south as irrational, sexually free, Dionysian, pagan, perverse, archetypally mother-bound due to an extravagant and extraordinary appeal of nature and climate, instinctive, irresponsible, lazy, cannibalistic. Are those projections still in operation? What was at first perceived by the *conquistadores* as heavenly, a paradisiacal projection, soon turned into a hellish project to steal, to usurp, and to abuse land and people in the Tropics—gold rush, wood traffic, slavery, soul mutilation.

In South America, "south" stands clearly for everything that is located below, repressed above, that which has always been seen from the North as *inferior* (as the early cartography exemplarily shows), intriguingly inviting on the way across the sea, a radical reversion to dark projections. This darkness has historically ranged from the Christian Hell of the missionaries to the mythological Hades of the psyche: inferior, unknown regions, a true underworld—land of the *inferiores*, of the serpent and the dragon.

In Brazil we are well aware of all this, for we start in the South. My main point here is that this archetypal "south" can be reimagined beyond Mediterranean culture. Brazilian syncretic polytheistic culture shines and, in itself, continues to offer a challenge for psychology regarding "south" as a cultural, ethnic, and imaginal location, a region of the soul beyond what has been already acknowledged as "south." It seems essential that the soul continues to be imagined, so I want to suggest that maybe *south* and *soul* have yet more in common beyond what Hillman showed us of value for psychology in Mediterranean classical culture. Cultures below the equator can help archetypal psychology continue to imagine even more radically its fundamental metaphorical direction.

Brazil is the largest Catholic country in the world; but it is as well a place where a polytheistic religion—the Afro-Brazilian religion of the Orixás—is alive and largely practiced every day with such a power that, unlike in other places, it also dwells strongly in urban areas, in the cities—psychotherapy's territory since the beginning. Brazil is a place where the division of monotheistic/polytheistic is in fact, and in psyche, no longer operative in a positive sense. The Afro-Brazilian polytheism (along with all its different ramifications) is very much alive *inside* the monotheism of the Christian official culture in Brazil, even though more conscious in some parts of the country than in others. Some speak here of paradox, others of tolerance or syncretism. Some attack this very syncretism, trying to purify influences, while others celebrate it. The psychological reality in Brazil indicates, anyway, this peculiar synthetic state of soul. This is a way of *south*.

How does all this affect and change the ways of a psychological *praxis*? How would this syncretic polytheistic culture offer a "place of practice" for psychology and psychotherapy regarding "south" as a cultural, ethnic, and imaginal location, again, a region of the soul?

One way to understand it is as an obvious result of the melting of the three absolutely different races that originally combined to form Brazilian people: the American Indian, the European Portuguese, and the African slave. *Coniunctio* as *solutio*. Black, white, and red. Miscegenation. And it is clear to me that *miscegenation* is the main contribution to psychology from Brazil. It offers a totally different style of consciousness, more inclusive and receptive, less abstract and conceptual. And it thus offers a chance to overcome what Hillman refers to as "white supremacy," that is, ego psychology, empiricism, subjectivism, spiritualism. Miscegenation represents a true descent into the "south."

Another aspect of this descent into south is to be found in the baroque. The baroque in Brazil, as in all South America, is not simply a transitory artistic movement imported from Europe and so attached to this origin and its canons. What the art historians insist is that, rather, the tropical baroque has to be understood in its own terms, as the first fully legitimate manifestation of art and culture to flourish outside Europe in the Colonies, one that has little to do directly with Europe, no longer a marginal artistic expression but something in itself. In fact, it is the first, original cultural manifestation in the South, and being so, I believe it will strongly reflect the very soul that was being formed in this "new" land. So it is part of a foundation. This "new soul"—or new step in the world soul-making—this mixture that was being engendered in Brazil through the encounter and mixing of three races begins to speak right here, right with the baroque. Brazilian baroque incorporates thus, apart from the European (Portuguese, Spanish, and Roman) elements, those from the Indian and Black influences. The baroque merges itself with many aspects of our deepest soul.

Opposed to the rationalist aspect of the Renaissance culture, the magical universe of the tropical baroque is rooted in the imagination—sensorial extremes of imagination. It is an art that can only be perceived in its full impact by the soul, not by the mind. The baroque, especially in Brazil, is the affirmation of fantasy as the deepest truth. It is a *contre-dance*, freedom to imagine, and it is the moment when we speak, not of a Re-naissance, but of a *naissance*, a birth, for the baroque, we all know, made possible independence (and not only for Brazil).

This baroque still defines, to this day, much of our soul. Our idea and experience of "south" is born under the sign of the baroque. So there is a latent "baroquism," so to speak, that continues to inform and characterize, deep down, much of the way Brazilians feel and live soul, south, and affection: the extremes of faith, the inclination to contradiction and ambivalence, the attraction for emotional vertigo, dance and festive ecstasy, the exaltation of the senses, the mystical impulse, aesthetic pleasure, tragedy, confusion, illusions of grandeur, the erotics of power and the power of erotics, the magic of words, excessive use of adjectives and, most of all, an image-sense, a sensibility for the image—this is all in the baroque. *Anima* phenomenology? Maybe. If so, then we have a rich soil for a psychology based on image to flourish, an imaginal psychology.

Our play with imaginal geography seeks to bring "south" *as an imaginal attribute in the world soul*, imagined as a move of soul-making, more soul-making, new soul-making.

PART V:

RESPONSIVE ENVIRONMENTALISM
THE SOUL OF THE CITY
IN DISTRESS

Joanne H. Stroud, Ph.D. in Psychology and Literature from the University of Dallas, lectures in Dallas, New York City, and Connecticut. She is a Founding Fellow of the Dallas Institute of Humanities and Culture, Director of Institute Publications, and editor of the Gaston Bachelard Translation Series, which consists of seven works on elemental imagination written by the French twentieth-century philosopher of science. The 2002 Bachelard Symposium she chaired in Dallas, "Matter, Dream, and Thought," attracted international attention. The series completion in 2011 was celebrated with a Bachelard Day on the 30th anniversary of the Dallas Institute. She served on the Board of Overseers of Harvard University for 12 years and serves on the Boards of the University of Dallas and the Southwestern Medical Foundation currently. She has taught literature and psychology and is author of *The Bonding of Will and Desire*; the four-volume series *Choose Your Element*; and *Time Doesn't Tick Anymore*. *Gaston Bachelard: An Elemental Reverie on the World's Stuff* and *Towers 2 Tall* were published in 2015.

JOANNE H. STROUD

Return of the Soul to the World

JAMES HILLMAN PINPOINTS, as no other philosopher or psychologist does, the current deplorable deadening of the awareness of the soul of the world, of the *anima mundi*. Hillman traces how the classical idea of the world as animated has been phased out during the last centuries by the erroneously inflated thought that humankind stands apart and can be separated from the health of our native planet. The concentration on the individual as isolated, the miasma that followed the Cartesian emphasis on humans as essentially thinking creatures, resulted in the present forgetfulness, unfortunately true even in psychology, that our surroundings have any influence on our personal problems. The fifty-minute therapy hour turned into an exploration concentrating only on relationships.

Hillman (2006) insists that the psychotherapist's job today needs to also involve "the examination of culture with a pathological eye" (p. 31). He quotes Robert Sardello's criticism of our current cultural life: "Our buildings are anorexic, our business paranoid. Our technology manic" (p. 31). The pathology of the world cries out for attention. Hillman aptly continues with this approach: "Depth psychology has insisted that the pathology of the world out there results simply from the pathology of the world in here" (p. 32). He characterizes the need for turning the entire practice of psychotheraphy on its head. This revolutionary move involves the realization that not only do we project upon the world our notions, but that the carelessness, the utilitarian approach to so many areas of our daily living (with utter disregard for the soul's needs) impinges upon our sense of well being. Therapy itself is less effective than it could be and will be lacking "until psychology admits the world into the sphere of psychic reality" (p. 32). Unconsciousness today emanates "not from repressed sexuality or familial relationships as much as *unconsciousness of things*" (p. 32, my emphasis). Later, in the chapter "The Cost of Ugliness," he reemphasizes this point: "So, the repressed today is not where we think it is, in our sexual feelings, racial prejudices, family knots, and hidden motives. Today the repressed is outside of us" (p. 197); shockingly, we live surrounded by a cemetery of dead things. Even our distrust of everything we eat, that it will somehow kill us, stems from the fallout of not honoring the living world.

Hillman pointedly directs our attention to a remembrance of the world soul of Platonism, which he notes, meant nothing less than the "world ensouled" (p. 33). To embrace this view, he advises: "re-enter the Platonic cosmos, which always recognizes that the soul of the individual can never advance beyond the soul of the world because they are inseparable" (p. 35).

How to raise consciousness of the world's soul? That query might be our mantra. Hillman defines "Aesthetic Sensitivity" as awakening of the heart's point of view:

> Awakening the imaging, sensing heart would move psychology itself from mental reflection toward cordial reflex. Psychology may then become again Florentine, for the move 'southward' that I have been urging these last twenty years . . . cannot be accomplished without moving as well the seat of the soul from brain to heart and the method of psychology from cognitive understanding to aesthetic sensitivity. . . .The move to the heart is already a move of *poeisis*: metaphorical, psychological (p. 37).

Furthermore, he adds, it is the appeal of what was once attributed to the goddess Aphrodite's sensual attraction that magnetizes our attention and care: "Aphrodite is the lure, the nudity of things as they show themselves to the sensuous imagination" (p. 40). With beauty as enticement, "each thing smiles, has allure, and calls forth *aisthesis*. 'Calling forth' provoking *kaleo*: this was Ficino's derivation of Aphrodite's main characteristic, *kallos*, beauty" (p. 38).

Kathleen Raine, the distinguished twentieth-century British poet and Fellow of the Dallas Institute, summarizes exactly the bonding of soul and beauty: "In the absence of beauty the soul is always in exile." In a review of Woody Allen's movie "Magic in the Moonlight," critic David Denby (2014) finds beauty as a hidden element: "Beauty—old beauty, permanent beauty—has become an emotional necessity in Allen's work." Hurrah, hurrah, glad to see the return to beauty! For so long, evoking beauty has been totally out of style.

This surprising advice comes from Hillman: shifting our focus of attention from head analysis to heart empathy would affect even the pace of living. In America in every walk of life everyone complains about lack of time. A desire to travel is in large part an attempt to find locations where time seems less pressured. He claims: "First, an aesthetic response to particulars would radically slow us down. To notice each event would limit our appetite for events. . . . Perhaps, as senses become refined, there is a scaling down of gigantism and titanism, those mythically perennial enemies—giants and titans—of culture" (p. 41).

Let us recognize the difficulty this switch in focus involves. All our schooling (especially, or more so, if you are of the female gender), all our experience has conditioned us to value mind over heart. Hillman offers this significant advice: "With the heart we move at once into imagination. For when the brain is considered to be the seat of consciousness we search for literal locations, whereas we cannot take the heart with the same physiological literalism" (p. 37). He adds, though: "We will not be able to move in this direction until we have made radical shifts of orientation so that we value soul before mind" (p. 48).

How do we address the issue of our insensitivity to our surroundings? Everywhere we see evidence of our disregard. We could not love the world and trash it as we do. Hillman details the hidden side of excessive consumption: "Every act of consumption is shadowed by its true cost and its shadow waste. . . . There is a shadow side to every act no matter how ideal, how hopeful, and progressive" (p. 310). In America our biggest export is waste material. Even outer space circling around our planet is filled with waste debris. Recently an ad for a Swiss bank proclaimed that in the future, waste will be energy. What a powerful thought! Is this the positive side of Einstein's famous equation?

Hillman invokes the Hippocratic maxim: "Before all else, above all, first, do no harm, harm nothing" (p. 351). Even our brightest ideas may have unforeseen consequences. Straightening the winding Trinity River in its flow through Dallas destroyed its life and turned the river into a garbage dump. Hillman warns that: "the Earth has its own virtues and forces: nature may be acting in ways that lack of caution does not let us see" (p. 351).

In addressing the city in distress, it took Hillman's final essay, "Ground Zero" in *City & Soul,* for me to appreciate fully the image of the tower. While investigating the images shared by the poet W. B. Yeats and C. G. Jung for my dissertation, I discovered a surprising coincidence—both of my favorite subjects chose to live in towers at almost the same time. Sometime around 1928, Yeats bought an Anglo-Norman tower and wrote a whole book of poems about its meaning for him, and Jung at Bollingen helped with the construction of one for his habitat. I thought, then, of the coincidence of these two towers and wondered: What does a tower mean? I am still puzzling what the urge toward ascension means and refer you (without too much self-promotion, I hope) to my book about towers, *Towers 2 Tall.*

Turning to the subject of the Twin Towers of New York City, Hillman suggests that Ground Zero "symbolizes a wound in the deep tissue of Western psyche" (p. 412). He further explains that we moved past the trauma of the millennium on January 1, 2000. It came and went without a hitch. The "Dragon Y2K" was slain. But we weren't really attentive to the masking of our fears of catastrophe. The "world-shattering, apocalyptic moment" happened one year later. "For what did not happen on 1/1/2000 did happen on 9/11/2001" (p. 404). The place itself that is called Ground Zero is "the physical center of the Zero moment in the change of consciousness, the place of the Twin Towers, their burning and their fall" (p. 404). Hillman contrasts this disaster to the "orrible torre" in Dante's *Inferno* with Ugolino imprisoned. The New York towers were extraordinary architectural splendors; some might say hubristic reminders of wealth and power, "towering magnificence of twentieth-century world commerce," both fallen. Were they emblematic of falling civilizations, such as T. S. Eliot's use of the tower image in "The Wasteland"?

Falling towers

Jerusalem   Athens   Alexandria

Vienna   London

Unreal. . . . (1998; p. 41)

But there is hope that we may yet learn, he reminds us: "For where there is pathology there is psyche, and where psyche, eros. The things of the world again become precious, desirable, and even pitiable in their millennial suffering from Western humanity's hubristic insult to material things" (p. 47).

We have thought the world's materiality exists only for our exploitation. Instead, Hillman notes, "As expressive forms, things speak; they show the shape they are in. They announce themselves, bear witness to their presence: 'Look, here we are!'" (p. 33). Indifference to our planet has consequences: "[W]e are heart-sick because we are thing-sick" (p. 38). He calls upon psychology to lift "the anesthetized stupor from our reactions, lift the repression in ugliness of things themselves" (p. 38). Things are where the soul now claims psychological attention and this awareness could be achieved with this new altered attitude: "Not only animals and plants ensouled as in the Romantic vision, but soul is given with each thing, God-given things of nature and man-made things of the street" (p. 33).

Let me suggest French philosopher Gaston Bachelard, as Hillman himself often does, for appreciation of our surrounding world. Bachelard, unusual for a man of science, points out how careful observation of the world's fabric sparks a love of the world. We need our aware thinkers to remind us of the *anima mundi*. Hillman gives a list of some: "*Anima mundi* reappears in further guises in 'the collective unconscious' in Jung . . . in the poetics of matter and space in Bachelard. . . And of course, ever and again in the great poets, specifically of this century in Yeats and Rilke, Williams and Stevens" (p. 48). Connective links and associations natural to the ever-dynamic poetic imagination won't allow us to forget the textures, the specialty of things. Indeed, again in Hillman's words: "soul differentiates by clinging to matter" (p. 411).

Hillman insists: "Psychic numbing, or anesthesia, is a major cause of environmental degradation, so that the awakening of primal responsiveness has become the first challenge for environmentalists" (p. 333). Isn't it confounding that environmental issues have so divided us? Don't all of us live here? He provides one possibility: the anti-ecological drive is an attempt to disregard the feminine, the earth—mother matter (p. 310). A wise man in India once proposed: How can one be mad at mother or mother earth who gave us birth?

"Responsive environmentalism aims to rekindle the natural urge that ties humans to habitat," and Hillman considers "awakening the aesthetic responses of the heart to be the first environmental task" (p. 332), adding "[t]he urge to engage, the sense of responsibility arising spontaneously in protest to ugliness, carelessness, and waste, and in defense of beauty and value shows that an aesthetic response is also political action" (p. 333).

Hillman summarizes how heart service with an attitude of urban ecology in our city life might narrow the gulf in imagination that separates inner feelings from outer places: "Service enlarges the relation of the City with Nature, transforms its feeling, softens its walls, its paranoia, so that citizens regard themselves, right in the midst of downtown doing their urban jobs, as serving the upkeep of the planet, in service to the wider world that is civilization and nature both, performing the greatest service possible—maintaining the continuity of this beautiful, this loveable planet" (p. 311). Amen. Namaste.

Indifference to our planet has consequences:

Hillman notes, . . .

"[W]e are heart-sick because we are thing-sick."

Scott Becker, Ph.D., is a clinical psychologist currently serving as the Acting Director of the Counseling Center at Michigan State University. Dr. Becker has published in *Spring* and *Death Studies*, and he contributed the psychological commentary to the recent biography *The Life and Ideas of James Hillman*. He is also the editor of the forthcoming *Inhuman Relations,* Volume 7 of the *Uniform Edition of the Writings of James Hillman*. Dr. Becker's areas of interest are informed by archetypal psychology and include trauma, mourning, dreams, multiculturalism, and astrology. He has also developed an integrative paradigm addressing the negative impact of technology and social media on neurological development and psychological functioning.

SCOTT BECKER

The Minotaur and the Matrix:
Technology and the Soulless City

ON THE CUSP of this new millennium, technology seems to have set us free. Everything and everyone is linked: we surf, text, Tweet, tag, Skype, Google, chat, poke, take selfies, and click hyperlinks, never pausing to reflect on the images embedded in this new language of speed and size and transcendence. We hit "like" for things that please us, and "dislike" for things that don't—with our thumbs up or thumbs down, each of us becomes a Roman emperor, each webpage and post a gladiator that lives or dies at our whim. But this seductive freedom has its shadow. We also live in a time of stolen identities; cyber-bullying; spy-cams, firewalls, and hackers; and relentless beeps, dings, buzzes, and ringtones. But the true paradox is that we live in a time of virtual connection and virtual isolation— all the world's our stage as we sit alone in the dark, staring at a glowing screen. This is the age of being linked in yet disconnected, of the inflated yet imprisoned ego, the iPod. We are kings of infinite space, bounded in a nutshell.

To these digital shadows that we all surely recognize, we need to add one that is darker and more obscure: Technology is changing everyone who uses it. A growing number of studies in the field of neurobiology suggest that our overuse of digital technology is quite literally altering the structure of our brains, and thereby our minds, our psyches, and our culture. From the micro-level of neurological development to the macro-level of social and political systems, digital technology is disconnecting us—from ourselves, from our relationships, from our cities and governments, and ultimately from the world itself, with the potential to render us indifferent to the world's suffering as well as our own. Our excessive use of digital technology—our literal, physiological addiction to it—appears to be inducing a dissociative, distracted, displaced, disembodied, disinhibited, and agitated state that is fundamentally not present, not here.

We are becoming more at home in the virtual world, the simulated city, than in our own. Here we would do well to remember the work of James Hillman on the importance of aesthetics for political awareness, expertly reviewed earlier here by Klaus Ottmann. If aesthetic perception is the source of our political sensibility and therefore our citizenship, then our dystopian nightmares on the cusp of this new millennium must now include the horrifying prospect of a thoroughly anaesthetized populace, a global population too distracted to notice, and too solipsistic and psychopathic actually to care that the world is on fire. We may be moving toward a horizon that includes the disturbing possibility of cities without actual citizens; cities without soul. In order to avert this disaster, we need to fully imagine it. We need to ask—what happens if our world collapses and no one cares? What if Eliot's vision fell short, and this is the way world ends, not with a whimper but a yawn? Or, in less literary but more vivid terms, what if our popular culture is obsessed with the zombie apocalypse because in a sense, we are the walking dead?

This lecture is too brief to do justice to the research that supports this bleak vision. So, for the sake of brevity—and after all, this is the age of bits and bytes—we will summarize the findings thematically. This summary lands us squarely in the labyrinth of neurobiology, and some of us may feel lost. But here is a clue as we wind our way through the maze; listen for the metaphors and images embedded in the literal, factual language.

First, our sleep is being eroded, both by the low-frequency light emitted by our back-lit devices and by the radio frequency received by our phones, because, as it turns out, our nervous systems function as antennae, and even as we try to sleep, we are tuned in. Those who move their phones away from the head of their bed report dreaming again.

Second, we are losing our capacity for sustained attention, concentration, comprehension, and memory. We are less able to integrate and contextualize information, and to recognize meaningful connections between facts and ideas. These deficits appear to be developing for a number of reasons, including changes in the structure of the frontal cortex and actual degradation of grey and white matter in critical areas of the brain.

Third, this thinning of neural connections is also occurring in the areas of the brain related to inhibition of socially unacceptable impulses and to empathy and relatedness. We are losing our ability to feel and understand others' experience, and the effect may be worse for adolescents and young adults. One study actually measured the capacity for empathy among college students as 40% lower than students of 20 or 30 years ago. We may be robbing coming generations of their capacity to feel, sacrificing them at the altar of technology and higher profits.

Hidden within this maze of information there is a central theme, a common thread: the idea of connection itself. All of the research cited here is consistent with the notion that we are losing the capacity to connect—to synthesize our thoughts and emotions, to maintain the mind-body connection, and to share our experiences with others, to feel their pain and their joy. This thread of connection, whether cognitive, emotional, or interpersonal, is a function of imagination, and the research suggests that we are beginning to lose that imaginal capacity, including our capacity to dream. As our thoughts become simpler, our memories become shorter, our hearts become colder, and our communication more fitful and shallow, we are at risk for what might be called collective soul-loss: losing our depth and complexity, and ultimately our passion, commitment, and communal feeling, along with our sense of belonging to something beyond ourselves.

Many years ago, in a documentary film, Hillman declared, "Now we realize that technology is our myth. . . ." The question then becomes, which myth is most relevant to our current dilemma? Each of us might make a different choice, but the one that informs this talk and that lies behind its rhetorical images—the labyrinth, the sacrifice of young people to monstrous greed, the thread of connection—is quite well known to us. We all recall the story of King Minos and the Minotaur, and of the hero, Theseus, who eventually slays the monster. Since we know this much of the story, and again for the sake of brevity, we will focus on two of the less-remembered characters: Daedalus and Ariadne.

To understand Daedalus' relevance, we need to highlight the darker side of his character by remembering the beginning of the story. Daedalus fled to the court of Minos following the murder of Perdix, Daedalus' nephew, who showed enough talent to threaten his uncle's pride, leading Daedalus to push his protégé off of a cliff. This image of Daedalus as a murderer is not often told, and it illustrates his affinity for King Minos.

The autocratic king and the clever technician share in their hubris; both refuse to sacrifice, to relinquish control. Technology, then, is not merely a tool misused by the powerful. The technical mind has its own thirst for power and its own innate ruthlessness, just as the ruling mind has a technical edge, using precise strategies for maintaining its power. Both styles, at their extremes, converge in the realm of psychopathy, of cold, calculating efficiency. The king and the technician are two sides of the same coin, joined in their craft. The more narrowly mechanical our thinking, and the more tightly we grasp the reins of power, the more we resort to Procrustean violence. Things must be just so, my way, at any cost. And so the technical and the ruling mind are able to collude in building a beautiful maze, concealing the beast within.

Ariadne is the daughter of Minos and Pasiphae, and as Carl Kerenyi has pointed out, she is closely tied to her half-brother, the Minotaur, whose original name is Asterion, the starry one, suggesting how quickly the stellar can become monstrous. Historically, images of Ariadne and Asterion were on two sides of the same Cretan coin, referencing both their kinship and the fact that Ariadne was the keeper of the labyrinth, forced to oversee the sacrifices made to the Minotaur. Upon meeting Theseus, however, Ariadne abandoned her duties out of love. It was her passion for Theseus that allowed him to escape the labyrinth by following a thread, also called a clue, ironically provided by Daedalus. But after their escape from Crete, Theseus abandons Ariadne in a cave and sails away, leaving us with an image of loss and betrayal.

In some versions of the story, there is a further descent. Ariadne, whose name means "most holy," is actually a goddess, the bride of Dionysos, and the cave in which she is abandoned is a shrine, dedicated to Dionysos himself. In outrage at her infidelity, Dionysos petitions Artemis to kill her, and she descends to the underworld, where she weds Dionysos and joins him in his cycle of death and rebirth, as god of the vine. In this sense, Ariadne was considered identical to both Aphrodite and Persephone, a lunar goddess of love, death, and resurrection.

So in the figures of Daedalus and Ariadne we have a remarkable narrative thread, one that winds its way from a selfish murder to romantic passion and betrayal to an underworld marriage to the Lord of Souls. What begins in narrowly vicious and calculated self-interest ends in ecstatic union with the divine, in the merging of life and death. What begins in Daedalus' and Minos' violent refusals to relinquish control ends in Ariadne's death and rebirth. In short, her abandonment leads to abandon.

What are we to take from this story? First, if we accept the notion that Daedalus and Minos are the dark figures who stand behind our current global power structure, the alliance of technocracy and plutocracy, we may recognize that future generations are being sacrificed in the name of progress, and we may awaken to a sense of outrage and the need for action. Closer to home, we may also recognize in ourselves the need to balance technical precision with compassion and moral conscience. We may awaken to our duty as global citizens to think, feel, relate, and act with courage and imagination.

In Ariadne's story we witness the power of human connection and passionate love, but the myth suggests that we need to move beyond the merely human. Heroic action and romantic love only take us so far. The pathway out of the maze leads to a place of despair, and ultimately to the realm of the dead.

Our way out of the self-serving, mechanical mind must follow a Dionysian path of divine madness, a return to the source of life that lies only on the other side of death. In terms of our present dilemma, this may not seem to be a practical idea; as we all know, Dionysos is not usually welcome in the city. But we already know his value. In fact, our appreciation for Dionysian excess is one of the reasons that we are all here. Our shared commitment to archetypal psychology, to the legacy of James Hillman, is at the heart of this conference, at the Institute that welcomed Hillman and his wild ideas when he was in search of a new home. We might go so far as to say that the city of Dallas can claim to be the only city to have welcomed Dionysos Mainolês, the mad, raging god, within its city limits, for after all, Hillman's method was less Apollonic than Dionysian.

There was, as Hillman once confessed, madness in his method, and we read him at our own peril–*caveat lector*. We went bugs, became tinged with pink madness, descended to Hades and Tartarus, flew to the dark side of the moon, succumbed to panic, sank with the Titanic, went blind with Oedipus, lame with Haephestos, and mad with the Maenads, were cursed by Hera, had our pockets picked by Hermes, suffered with Psyche, got burned with Eros, lost our white innocence, felt our souls bake, blacken, and bruise, felt our reason fail, our egos die, our idols fall, our wings melt, our hopes turn to ashes. Seen through this alchemical lens, this conference becomes an extension of reading his work as an exercise in transformation. In submitting to Hillman's work, we join him in the crucible, the acid bath, the grave. We become the worker and the material both. In reading Hillman, we follow Socrates and practice dying. As Auden (1975) said, "The crack in the tea-cup opens / A lane to the land of the dead" (p. 132). Perhaps along this path lies a way out of our technological labyrinth. Today we will leave that path open, avoiding the trap of a social program or a political revolution. For now, it may be enough to imagine that our technical problem has a soulful solution.

... we are losing the capacity to connect—to synthesize our thoughts and emotions, to maintain the mind-body connection, and to share our experiences with others, to feel their pain and their joy.

—Scott Becker

Now we realize that technology is our myth....

—James Hillman

Robert Sardello, Ph.D., is co-founder and co-director of The School of Spiritual Psychology, which began in 1992, and co-editor of Goldenstone Press. He is author of six books. His main emphasis has been to develop theoretical and practical approaches to perceiving and being in right relation with the soul of the world, showing that humans are pulled from the time stream from the future rather than pushed from the past, and developing the interior consciousness of the heart. He has created new, yet very practical cultural visions in areas such as the meaning of books, the essence of service, the virtues, money, business, giving, healing, religion, living through the heart, and how to be in right relationship with and in the earth. He is an independent teacher and scholar. He is a Founding Fellow of the Dallas Institute of Humanities and Culture.

ROBERT SARDELLO

Between Greed and Grief:
The Imaginal Space of the City

IN APPLYING ARCHETYPAL PSYCHOLOGY to imagining "City and Soul," the inherent 'Pathologizing' of soul described by James Hillman stands as a crucial dimension needing attention. Cities tend to try to 'build' the pathological dimension out, or to gentrify true soul regions in the name of improvements, and often a more or less sentimental imagination of soul display occurs, resulting in literalizing city and soul according to what one hopes for the city rather than soul appearing within and as city.

I am going, in this brief talk, to outline an archetypal imagination of the destiny of America. It is an inherently pathologized destiny. You will see how this destiny shapes the way cities are built. Hopefully we can see, through bringing the soul of the city into relation with the soul of the nation, some aspects revealing how cities might meet their unfolding in ways that bring awareness into the deep destiny of this country while also altering the imagination of cities.

One archetypal revelation of the spiritual destiny of America begins with this unusual legend. When Jesus was born, the youngest of the three Magi, whose name was Amesis, looked into the eyes of this child and saw the possible future of the human being. He saw that it is possible that every human being could live in complete harmony with the earth and with the cosmos and with each other. This reality was inherent in the eyes of the child. And Amesis saw that the future of the human being had to do with the destiny of the land of America.

Amesis came to what is now America, traveling by way of Alaska. He came to a region now known as High Tor, in New York, a place located right above what is now the Tappen Zee bridge, outside New York City. You can see Manhattan from this high place.

Amesis knew that the destiny of America involved soul's encounter with the spirits of greed. The indigenous people of this region had 'handled' the presence of these beings by using magical means to keep them held within the earth, unable to escape.

Amesis came to this place where this imprisonment occurred. He knew that we would have to encounter these spirits to complete the destiny of America and hoped to transform them into spirits of good. He set up an altar and stayed there for a very long time. He married an Indian woman and daily did ritual at this altar. One day the spirits emerged, but they were far, far more powerful than could be imagined. A huge explosion occurred, creating the Hudson Valley and the Hudson River. The spirits of greed were released for the first time.

A hint of what we are still required to confront within soul as we build this country into its cities can be heard in two images of the Hudson. The Hudson River originates in a very small, very pristine lake high in the Adirondacks. The name of this lake is Tear of the Cloud Lake. Then, the Hudson River itself is a huge estuary. This means that the salty water of the sea comes up the river to meet the tears coming down. The sea flows up as far as Troy, New York, a distance of 150 miles. We can imagine the Hudson as a river of tears—originating from the tears of the highest cosmos and the deepest ocean.

A second legend can be found in the book *Rocklandia: History and Legends of Rockland County, New York*, which is the location of High Tor. It is called the "Legend of the Salamander."

Several centuries ago, a group of Rosicrucian alchemists came to High Tor under the leadership of Hugo—a name that means 'bright of mind.' They too came to transform the spirits of greed. They set up a forge for purifying iron at the site. High Tor is a region plentiful in iron. Much of the iron that built early Manhattan came from this region. The tailings of the mines can still be found there.

Iron becomes steel by purification and by reheating, altering brittleness into something malleable and strong. The reheating strengthens it; that is, placing this metal into human hands imbues it with purely earthly human will, now combined with the archetypal power of iron, Mars. The iron from this region, coming from deep within the earth of the place of imprisonment of the beings of greed, brings iron, greed, and city development into imaginal cohesion.

The tale is long and complex, so I have to present only the barest of outlines.

The group of alchemists set up a forge and began purifying iron. Two workers constantly watched the fire. The forge had to be shut down for a while every seven years; otherwise, there is danger that the salamander, the elemental being of fire, will be released. Hugo's son, also named Hugo, is one of the watchers, and he was so driven by this alchemical task that he refused to shut the forge down. As they looked deep into the earth-fire, they saw what seem to be gemstones lining the depths of the earth, and at the very bottom of the fire, there was a large salamander with a golden triangle on its back, and within the triangle they saw a code. They were inwardly told that anyone who can read the code would have all the wealth that they could ever imagine, and thus these watcher alchemists lost the purity of their intention, as does the father Hugo.

The father Hugo also had a daughter, Mary. She was exceptionally pure of heart, extremely sensitive, barely able to engage in the will needed for earthly existence.

One day, when the time for closing the forge had long gone by, son Hugo's attention was entirely captured by the salamander and he tried to speak the code word on the back of the salamander. Hugo's father came to the forge and became equally enthralled. The fire became dangerously hot. The elder Hugo's wife ran to the forge and sprinkled water on it, hoping to drown out the fire. There was an explosion, and she and the son Hugo were killed.

The elder Hugo wandered off, seemingly crazed by what had happened. The daughter, Mary, was left to live alone. Then one day a beautiful young man appeared. She and the young man fell in love. Their completely pure, spiritual love remained unconsummated.

Then, the elder Hugo returned. He saw his daughter, Mary, with the young man, and in his delirium he thought that the young man was responsible for all the tragedy that occurred here, and he grabbed him to throw him into the fire. Just as he begins to fall into the pit, the young man, due to the purity of love he holds for his beloved, instead ascends. This young man, who may also actually be the salamander, is a "good" fallen archangel who had been given the task of bringing some capacities to earth for the sake of all of humanity. He became entranced with the earthly realm, and in attempting to unite with it, did not complete his spiritual task. We cannot help but feel that this fallen archangel was to bring the capacity to deal in the right way with greed. Instead, the forces of archetypal greed are released into the world.

These two legends both take place in that region that overlooks Manhattan. The next upheaval through this location of the spirits of greed takes place as the famous Manhattan Project.

During the Manhattan Project, Manhattan became the scene for the preparation of the atomic bomb. The scientific research took place at Columbia University. Buildings all over Manhattan became the secret headquarters for working out the details. The Kress skyscraper served as the command headquarters. Stockpiles of uranium were kept on Staten Island. Robert Oppenheimer grew up in a family of great wealth in Manhattan. His home was filled with art and his mother hoped Robert would be an artist. He became the physicist of the atomic bomb.

The atomic bomb, the culmination of the Manhattan Project, was exploded on July 16, 1945, at a place with the code name of "Trinity," near Socorro, New Mexico. The bomb is 'anti-Trinity,' and one that releases even deeper forces that assist the spirits of greed. You recall that at the moment of the explosion of the bomb, Robert Oppenheimer says: "Now I become Death, destroyer of worlds." That is, the ego, which is the potential of the I AM of life, turns into the I AM of death. Our very identity as human beings now serves the forces of death. And the American destiny sidetracks into addictiveness to destruction. Perhaps the most human of all soul capacities, that of grieving, turns into emotional expression of loss, something to be overcome as soon as possible. This most basic of soul capacities, deeply felt all the time, reminds us of mortality. Greed attempts to deny this soul capacity.

The explosion turned a square mile of the New Mexico landscape into an eerie kind of green glass, now named Trinitinite. No life takes place there. The bomb formed a vast "black hole" that sucks in the true destiny of America so that the forces of greed become stronger and stronger.

Archetypally, this explosion reaches deep down into the Underworld, there in New Mexico, touching into and joining with the forces of the Aztec gods. The explosion touches into that archetypal impulse of removing the heart from the human being, that is, removing the capacity of creative imagination to make a world; without the imaginal heart, greed meets no resistance.

The religious authorities in Aztec life saw the human being as in a continuous state of debt toward the gods. The sun that sheds light for the good of the human demands recompense. The Aztecs of that time made evil supreme by devising a dualistic worldview and painting evil as the good to be attained—the killing of innumerable people, and tearing out the heart and offering it to the gods. This reversal of good and evil is enacted now in our world by placing materialism as the supreme good to be attained. This goal, emerging since the days of the occurrences at High Tor, requires the dualistic separation of good from evil, and then reversing which is which. Spiritual greed tears out the imaginal heart.

The fourth and most recent upheaval showing the unfolding of the union of the spirits of greed with the spirits of darkness occurs on 9/11/2001. Here we see the forces of greed taking advantage of this reversal of the forces of good and evil. In the aftershock of terrible grief, we were told to continue living, to go out and shop, to go to Disneyland. The directive of the president of the United States marks the moment of the unleashing of the forces of greed full force into the world, because now we are convinced in soul that greed is good.

There is much to be imaged with 9/11. Mystery and controversy still surround this tragedy and thankfully keep the imaginal aspect alive. It is not a simple and uncontested fact that America was attacked by terrorists. The heat from the explosion was intense, and the iron remained molten for weeks, when, if the collapse of the buildings was due to the implosion, the heat would have subsided in days. Many engineers have said that the collapse of the buildings and the fires could not have been due to the impact of the airplanes.

A fault line runs in the region of the twin towers, and an earthquake of magnitude 4.5 occurred in New York City in 2000. That fault line runs up toward High Tor. These imaginal pictures reveal the continued unfolding of the legend of the destiny of America. We can imagine the 9/11 event as an upheaval, very direct, of the spirits of evil, and only secondarily a literal attack.

Greed accelerated exponentially since the explosion of greed on 9/11. The stock market continues to soar. So does corruption in the realm of finances, spilling over into the government. The addiction to destruction shows everywhere, most visibly in a government with political parties unable to even pretend civility. The division between greed and grief, an archetypal image that is one, not two, seems now nearly completed, and shows up as divided cities of steel skyscrapers and financial centers and wealth and incredible corruption, which everyone sees and cannot stop, divided from our grief, which unmet, becomes violence in the world. We cannot stop the greed because it now lives autonomously, divided from soul regions of unrecognized grieving, which is the formula for untold violence, for violence lives as untended grieving.

Another region of New York also bears the name of that High Tor. It lies in upstate New York, north of Rochester, at the edge of Lake Ontario. This region holds the memory of Hiawatha, who brought peace to the five warring tribes, bringing about the Iroquois Nation. The region was named "Mannahata" by the native Americans, from which the name "Manhattan" derives. The name means something like "the point of land at the region of the tumultuous waters of the beings of destruction."

The great initiate, Dekanawida, born of a virgin, crossed Lake Ontario and came to America in a white granite boat. The boat symbolizes going across this lake as going through the Underworld. He assigned Hiawatha, who at the time was among the warring tribes, and was a cannibal, to bring peace to the five warring nations. Hiawatha—a name meaning 'he who combs snakes out of the hair'—an image of bringing 'clarity of seeing' into the world—undergoes incredible grieving as he travels from tribe to tribe to try to convince them to live in peace. His wife and three daughters and a child of one of the daughters are brutally killed as Hiawatha persists with his task.

As Hiawatha wandered in deep grief, somewhat comforted by the life and beauty of nature, he walked by a lake filled with ducks. The ducks all of a sudden took flight, and all of the water of the lake was taken up with them. He walked through the bed of the lake and saw the many empty shells and picked them up and made them into strings of beads, which become 'wampum.' Wampum never originated as a form of money or trade. A group of Dutch immigrants began introducing this practice on Long Island, right across from Manhattan.

As Hiawatha continued to speak with the warring tribes, he now sat with them, and they shared stories of grieving, and Hiawatha gave each person who shared their grief a string of beads, beads holding the archetypal powers of unification.

The two High Tor stories bring back into original archetypal union what remains separated, keeping the destiny of the nation confused and the future of the soul of the city uncertain. Greed forms a tandem, a syzygy, with grief. The split colors every archetypal pattern imaginable with greed—spiritual greed, greed for power, money greed, and most of all ego-greed, the fantasy that every archetypal presence is about us, the idealism of the city turned into rampant me-ilism—my power, my money, my possessions, my grief. . . and all the rest. Archetypal presence creates individual character and makes character beyond anything personal and therefore potentially creative.

Suppose we grieve our money-greed. It is not a matter of rejecting or imagining money as "evil." Instead, we grieve money, become present to the inner knowing that money is not energy as is currently imagined, but rather the blocking of energy when we hold to the notion that it is ours and is something we must have to exist and that money is held in the imagination of scarcity because an archetypal reality has become someone's ego-possession. Money-greed enslaves humanity. Separating greed from grief in the realm of money closes possibilities, forms the fear of 'not enough, never enough,' and separates one person from another.

Grieving money awakens the true imagination that money is not necessary for life. Without money the value of everyone is equal and we can imagine the city as being made according to the unique contribution of everyone and according to the needs of everyone. The same creativity of imagination opens up when the greed—of everything—opens to the archetypal presence of grieving—grieving power, grieving knowledge, grieving helping, grieving anything that catches us in the imagination of possessing. Then we can begin to see that the city concerns people, we might say archetypally free people because the fullest range of imagination is free to work through us, where visions become reality, where people are recognized for whatever contribution they are able to make to the community.

What if we begin, then, living in the imaginal space between greed and grieving in relation to everything, not just money? The archetype itself clarifies and is not confused by still thinking in terms of two realities—greed and grieving. We begin to live the imaginal space of the city as the simultaneous presence of plentitude and emptiness. The archetypal image exists and is all around and within us; we have just not noticed it.

More Conversations

Two papers were not presented at the 2014 symposium; they are added here to our explorations.

Urban Renewal

TOM CHEETHAM

Longing for Ugliness

JONATHAN HARRELL

Tom Cheetham, Ph.D., is the author of five books on the imagination and the meaning of Henry Corbin's work for the contemporary world. He is a Fellow of the Temenos Academy in London and Adjunct Professor of Human Ecology at the College of the Atlantic in Bar Harbor, Maine. He lectures regularly in Europe and the U.S.

TOM CHEETHAM

Urban Renewal

Grace to be born and live as variously as possible.
—Frank O'Hara (2008), "In Memory of My Feelings"

1. Pictures of Nothing

IN THE SPRING OF 2003 the charismatic and controversial art historian and curator Kirk Varnedoe delivered the Mellon Lectures in Fine Art at the National Gallery in Washington.[1] He called the series "Pictures of Nothing: Abstract Art Since Pollock." Over the course of six consecutive Sundays he outlined an argument for the importance of abstract art in a pluralistic democracy. He spoke with excitement, animation, and passion every week and concluded with what he well knew was his final public appearance on that last Sunday afternoon just three months before he died of cancer at the age of 57. While listening to the audio files of these remarkable and moving talks and then reading the edited transcript, which was published in the Bollingen Series (2006), I was struck again and again by the feeling that what he was up to had a lot in common with James Hillman's work, but in quite a different context.

Varnedoe was dismissive of the stock categories of art historical criticism. He had little patience for any of the standard "-isms." The works themselves always overflow the concepts we use to describe them. Rather than aiming for a grand, unified analysis, he preferred multiple, overlapping, and simultaneous readings, and argued that a process of endless creative interpretation is essential to the experience and the creation of modern art. The works themselves are often interpretive responses to creations that came before. This vision of a ceaseless conversation and flow of interpretation mirrors Henry Corbin's approach in the realm of theology. Corbin proposed a "perpetual hermeneutics" of sacred texts, suggesting a grand alliance between literature and religion. Varnedoe confirms my belief that all the arts must be included in this partnership. But more than this, both Hillman and Varnedoe thought that this principle of indeterminacy denying us the possibility of any final or universal truth applies across the full spectrum of human culture. Varnedoe said,

> Modern art writ large presents one cultural expression of a larger political gamble on the human possibility of living in change and without absolutes. . . .There is only bottomless debate, fragmented and plural consensus, with overlapping edges that evolve through history with no fixed goal. . .what we are about in culture is getting better locally, with no idea of any final best.[2] (p. 270)

143

At the core of this shared sensibility lies a fundamental delight in a rich and never-ending process of exploration and discovery.

One aspect of Varnedoe's account of abstract art stands out for me. As with Hillman's psychology and Corbin's theology, his vision is founded on a deep faith in the power of not knowing. Of abstract art he said,

> this is an art that, by its very nature, willfully and knowingly flirts with absurdity and emptiness, dancing on the knife edge of nonsense and beckoning us to come along. . . Abstraction. . . is a recurrent push for the temporarily meaningless. . . [It requires an act of faith] in possibility, a faith not that we will know something finally, but a faith in not knowing, a faith in our ignorance, a faith in our being confounded and dumbfounded, a faith fertile with possible meaning and growth. (p. 271)

The emergence of meaning requires an empty space for exploration. Moreover, the longer we can hold ourselves in doubt and uncertainty, the greater will be the rewards. Varnedoe (2003) puts it this way: "Abstract art is most successful when the reach for meaning seems the longest and most uncertain, embracing a great range of intuitions barely imaginable before the work was done" (part 5, "Satire, Irony, and Abstract Art"). It is in that liminal state of unknowing that intuitions arise and we extend ourselves outward into the unknown. I find the central idea in Varnedoe's lectures right here. He says, "The abstract artist may colonize a new realm of feeling" and by so doing "rejigger a new base alphabet within which a great number of others can represent the world in very different ways." On this account, abstraction is perhaps freer than any other form of art in fulfilling one fundamental, creative function of all art: to extend the range of our feeling and perception.

2. An Urban Imagination

Looking at the works Varnedoe used to illustrate his talks, I was struck by how urban it all felt—how much abstract art seems a phenomenon of the modern city. I have long thought of myself as a country boy. I grew up in what was then rural Connecticut, and I now live in the woods in rural Maine, for the most part contentedly. Somewhere in his writings Hillman happily points out that his name suggests a nomadic, rustic disrupter of centralized powers, a "hill man." I felt a little smug a few years back when I discovered that my name conjures a wild lineage too, "cheet" being a rare survival from the old Celtic meaning "forest," and "ham" from the Anglo-Saxon for "dwelling." So I was slightly surprised when a recent flood of poems, which I wrote more or less during the weeks that I was listening to Varnedoe, was full of cityscapes and urban adventures and the rhythm and pace of city life. I wondered about these two mysterious activities of the creative imagination, abstract art and poetry: What is urban about the un-knowing that might link them?

We live in a world dominated by city culture as never before in human history. Even those who live in the woods are immersed in cultural phenomena that have their origins in cities. Our experiences are radically different, not only from those of the precious few remaining inhabitants of the real wilderness but also from those of rural people, and even city people of only a few decades ago. The City is everywhere. Varnedoe (2003) says we seek affirmation of a sense that our lives are different from everything that came before, that life is now more complex than has yet been articulated, and that we are willing to endure disori-entation and the destruction of cherished norms in the search for the affirmation of our particular experiences. "Abstract art," he writes, "reflects the urge to push toward the limit, to colonize the borderland around the opening onto nothingness, where the land has not been settled, where the new can emerge" (part 5, "Sat-ire, Irony, and Abstract Art"). The numbing complexity and intense disorientation that presses us to the limits of the known almost on a daily basis is profoundly urban. Modern cities are places where meanings and feelings are most intensely concentrated, confusing, and complex and therefore where new experiences are nearly unavoidable and where a dizzying range of unknowns are simply there to be encountered. But we are adaptable creatures, and it is possible and even prob-ably essential that we become desensitized to some of this. Longtime city dwellers don't experience things this way. To them the city seems perfectly natural. It is the outsider, the awestruck rural visitor, who is most disoriented. I think that disorien-tation, confusion, and a sense of homelessness provide one way of enabling the creation of new forms of meaning and feeling.

This is complex terrain even if we stay anchored in abstract art in Amer-ica. There is a world of difference between the experience of making sense of minimalist works of the '60s, where there seems to be literally nothing to get hold of, and struggling in the chaos of one of Cy Twombly's enormous mytho-logically themed paintings, which are so full of mysterious dynamisms it seems miraculous that they stay on the wall. But in either case it is the move into un-knowing and, most important, into confused and inarticulate feeling that is so disorienting, even frightening, and so potentially creative about the experience. The same is true in the more challenging arts. It is part of what drives me to write poetry and to venture into the freedom and strangeness of the unknown. That opening into the not-yet-felt is perhaps the very essence of what makes poetry poetic. It is certainly what makes it creative—what creative imagination is about. In my experience, this border crossing, stepping repeatedly into the unknown and unspeakable and back home again to safer ground, is exactly the experi-ence of becoming conscious of a complex. Many years ago my analyst asked me about my unwilling journeys into some rather terrible depths, "What does it feel like when you are there, in those places?" There was absolutely nothing I could say—I had no words for those feelings. I was not merely homeless, but violently unhoused in a foreign land where my native language and my strategies for coping were utterly useless. That is what it is like to be unconscious. In a less extreme way, poetry can lead us into the unknown. So can much modern art. Precisely by being less extreme this art, perhaps, helps us prepare for more difficult travels. If we pay attention, such works can help expand our consciousness. They can extend and articulate our feelings and give us a new base alphabet, a new language.

By awakening us to the borderlines of the unknown that lie just below the surfaces of things these arts can help us escape the numbness, habituation, and inattention that come with repetition and familiarity. It is dangerous to become too comfortable. We stop paying attention, and then the naturally subtle depth, fluidity, and mystery of immediate experience elude us. Poetry and the arts can reawaken us to the strangeness of the world. They force us to notice things anew, to achieve what the Zen Buddhists call beginner's mind. I'll recount one modest example of this kind of encounter with meaninglessness and suggest this kind of thing can happen anywhere, in any context, in every conceivable modulation of intensity from the most evanescent to the nearly unendurable.

Alex Katz is an American painter who has worked in New York since the 1940s and was a friend of many of the prominent New York poets and of most of the abstract expressionist painters. Though not himself really an abstractionist, Katz's work is very spare and simple. I never liked it. It seemed to me merely silly—even meaningless. The paintings just hung there, huge and mute. But when I discovered that Frank O'Hara and John Ashbery, both sophisticated art critics whose poetry I am very fond of, had known Katz and admired his painting, I thought I ought to look once more. Katz has lived in Maine every summer for sixty years, and Colby College, which is in the town where I work, has an enormous gallery of his paintings, and so I spent a long time there last winter and spring. One day in June something suddenly clicked, and I was startled as those paintings began to open up for me. My God, I thought, there is so much to look at! And immediately I wanted someone to talk to about it—the paintings and I were becoming articulated together; I found that we all suddenly had something to say.

To make these crossings into the open, you have to be willing to leave the house. Sometimes it requires something drastic to get yourself out. This brings us right into the chaotic, archaic ferment of the eternal and ever-changing city. Jasper Johns called Frank O'Hara a modern Hermes carrying messages among poets and painters. He was the quintessential New York poet. He wrote in "Meditations in an Emergency," "I can't even enjoy a blade of grass unless I know there's a subway handy" (2008, p. 66). Surely his love of modern art was fused with his passion for the city in all its chaos, excitement, mystery, diversity, and change. His friend William Weaver was with him one day as they passed some old brownstones being demolished. As Weaver recalls, "I said, in the usual clichéd way, 'Oh what a pity they're tearing down those brownstones.' Frank said, 'Oh no, that's the way New York is. You have to just keep tearing it down and building it up'" (qtd. in Gooch, 1993, p. 218).

I can't even enjoy a blade of grass

unless I know there's a subway handy.

– Frank O'Hara

NOTES

[1] Varnedoe was a MacArthur Fellow in 1985 and taught at Stanford, Columbia, and New York University, and was for thirteen years the chief curator of painting and sculpture at the Museum of Modern Art in New York, and then Professor of the History of Art at the Institute for Advance Study at Princeton.

[2] As Adam Gopnick points out in the forward to *Pictures of Nothing*, Varnedoe owes a great deal to the American pragmatist philosopher Richard Rorty.

Jonathan Harrell is part-time professor of English at Collin College and Manager of Operations at the Dallas Institute of Humanities and Culture. He received his M.F.A. in Poetry from the University of Alaska at Anchorage. In January 2014, a selection of his poems, entitled "Masculinear," appeared in the literary journal *Assaracus*.

JONATHAN HARRELL

Longing for Ugliness

IN *CITY & SOUL*, James Hillman (2006) writes, "...our problems originate not only in our private selves and their pasts, but are reactions to our public spaces, . . . and habitations, our psychic interiority and interior design are deeply correlated, much as it was believed for centuries that the soul of the person and the *anima mundi* or soul of the world are inseparable" ("The Cost of the Ugly," p. 196).

In order to avoid delving into the digital numbness or accepting the radical notion that architecture cannot deaden us, we can escape the wrath of incorporeal Beauty and lift off of and out of our prisons of edifice and psychology, leaving our souls to convalesce with the prostrate Soul of the Earth for a time; that we might return purified and reawakened.

Our bodies are not so different from the edifices we see, every day, driving through the City. Like them, we are told, *you are this. Because I say you are this.* Even when we feel like we are not that, whatever, that, may be. Old. New. Ugly. Beautiful. Dumb. Intelligent. Single-use. Multi-use. Or if we are lucky, somewhere in the middle. *You are that. And then, I am this.*

We resist. We strike out on new roads and form new cities.

We try to find more gravity as imagination departs. In a sense, we try to extoll Beauty's largesse upon what we make as if it is that simple. We scroll the mouse over to the search engine and type in "Beauty." Something effervescent arises. Pictures of paradise. Families at Christmas. Puppies splashing in a swimming pool. Ancient art. We print it and post it. Some might not call it ugly-making, the virtual Sanskrit that hangs no weight on us. We are observers and gatherers in a fiber-optic era. Of Beauty, that we cannot be certain, but something pops up if we ask for it.

Perhaps, more than we might have at first believed, we start to see our skin as a wall against the world, something that contains our elements and us. And we come to understand what moves inside of the edifice. Or we try to understand it. Some call it the Soul. Some just call it a brain and its psychology. It is something physical and maybe something spiritual; the metaphysical. The private island of mercurial understanding; of distant but relative calm. The stormless center of ourselves, where our light is colored to greet us.

Hillman (2006) suggests that when we repress our reaction to environment, we encourage soul to become despondent from brain, and thus to demystify the imaginal locus of existence and name each day simply a physical experience (p. 197). Never mind with the fuzz and intemperance of metaphysics. Soul flees and we flee to cyberspace. But that space is empty. Similarly, imaginations are becoming vast, refracted annals.

Maybe the soul *should be* a private language, a language hidden in the diasporas, fleeing, always, from being found. And so the soul of the City must also pulse somewhere "out there," dancing in the midnights of our dreaming, among the starlit tympani of letters being written, again, on us, and the letters we have written upon it. "For repression is never where we believe it lies" (p. 197). It sits flat against the walls of restaurants and highway overpasses. In our searching for self, we have been searching for the City's true face, looking everywhere for it. Around every new bend there is opportunity, life, and potential. We start fresh and grow a tree in our yard. A child in our home. We invent anew our spirit's journey and venture forth into the skin, in the true face of the self. Into the City. Into culture. Into the classroom. Into poetry. And perhaps into Beauty.

It may be true that the classroom is the last bastion where imagination can retain its gravitas. The students turn off the cell phones. The mind becomes the keyboard, the mouse, and the screen. The piece of paper is where the search results must be originated, not found. The City: it provides for us in the classroom what history has hemorrhaged; the truth of imagination that is not easy to experience in the architecture of binary code. The planning for tomorrow is simply that in order to be influenced by our surroundings, we must first surrender our repression to the Ugly truth we have been ignoring: this world, for the most part, is not being seen, experienced, and felt. Rather, it is being recorded, videotaped, and photographed. What we can touch we would rather retouch; what we can see we would rather reframe; and what we can imagine we would rather reduce in order to reveal.

As Hillman writes, "So long as education in beauty and awareness of ugliness is considered accessory to making a living, that is, accessory to making a life, music appreciation, rhetoric and elocution, poetry and drama, studio hours that open the eye and instruct the hand will also be elective, accessory, not core to the curriculum because not core to the culture" (p. 198).

You are strong, we say to the City. Magnificent, like the pouring down rain on asphalt in late August. Steam rising forth among the tailpipes, and through Your windows, upon Your face, which, like a doorway, is pushed open slightly by the humidity. But You breathe out Your own exhaust, Dallas, and You breathe it in. An acrid chambering ego is pouring forth from You with its intertwining guilt and forgiveness. This strength You possess is not intelligence, is not beautiful. It is an elective identity feeding into a machine; the machinery of "making a living."

You must be patient, we say to the City. Don't pretend to know what You do not or feign understanding when You are confused. Listen to music from cars and relax as they drive down the roads of You, enjoying Your many grand edifices, the monuments to will and ambition, to service and to calling; to Your Beauty and yes, to Your Divine Ugliness. Feel able to bear witness to life as a citizen of the greater planet of cities, with humility and grandiloquence. But question technology. As they sit in offices and speak to one another on phones, and email and text with levity and with brevity, turn to them. In all of it, in the massive digital anachronism sputtering forth into this new century from the robotic dispossessed stratosphere of longing for Beauty, long for Ugliness instead. Long for their ugly senses of justice, of camaraderie. And the glory shall be Yours in the ratty old carports where they hide their trashy little secrets.

You will vacillate between the knowing and the burdening, either in it or feeling it from without. And the soul energies will release and bless You, and contend with emotions like Samaritans. They will want for Your passion and for Your longing too. And for Your verve they will push out onto and into You; onto Your walls and into Your waterways. Like a Scripture of the wasting away, dumped as a velvet bag of bones on the soft unspeaking loam of the Earth on which even You reside, You will hear from them the common choruses of their commutes.

"We need to see where we are going."

"We need to hear new music frequently."

"We need to know ahead of time what we should not do so we will not feel what we do not have to feel."

You are the metaphor and the thing itself, Dallas. You are emboldened by Your profundity. Gravity holds You and releases You. You release and hold gravity. As Hillman writes, "It costs ugliness to awaken our contemporary anesthetized consciousness" (p. 203).

What protects us against our very own repression is a repression of experience with the City. We can prepare to restore the Soul to the City by first casting it out, in real time, the same way we have been trained by technology to accept Ugliness. For the work we have to do requires re-entry into our common spaces without the prejudice of modern affectations. When we allow ourselves to reject the virtuosity of technology's dangerous convenience, we learn to recognize its danger lies in its equalizing force, in its ability to stabilize us and string us along its frequency of paroxysmal immediacy. We learn to realize that we are not all equal just as we know we are not all Beautiful. Therefore, everything must not look beautiful. For what is a binary system without its poles?

According to Hillman, we can live in

> an open society of equality based on equal access, for each one can have his and her computer and thereby interact with anyone anywhere as well as accumulate a vast bank of data.
>
> Sitting there, booted up, right hand on the mouse, in control of this treasury of opportunity, what is the cost, what is the loss—since for every gain something is always lost?
>
> First, the body… You're in touch with everything in the world but your own physical self. (pp. 200-01)

But what of that self which is being lost? Losing the physical self is hard to conceive of when we can still touch our own bodies. However, is it not easier to conceive of the loss of the physical world as it relates to those "things" we make with our bodies? In the aggrandizement of human intellect that is in theory providing to us equal yet virtual access to all of the "things" we have been making and have made, what specific elements of Beauty are we losing? Hillman would argue that "the cost of electronic miracles may well be more ugliness; the loss, poetry" (p. 202).

Cities fortify as souls. If the classroom is where Beauty is restored and poetry returns as a physical artifact of the pre-virtual, the technologically repressed classroom offers an insular experience with place as an imitation of Soul rather than an externalized commodity of the imagination. It gains weight and can be resurrected in the minds of students through experience with place. In the classroom that rejects technology, either out of necessity or intentionally, and one wherein the professor leads students away from the hyper-redundancy of checking email, updating Facebook, and texting, Beauty burns and Ugliness rises. The City strengthens.

As an adjunct professor of English at a community college, I am often reminded that many believe Beauty does not live in a cinder block palace like my classroom; Beauty possesses itself with earnestness and with a willful pursuit of enlightenment. Mediocrity breeds "ugliness," or a perpetual spiraling down into the impoverished mind. Beauty, thus, has been transmogrified into Ugliness at my college because my college is "ugly." Like C.S. Lewis' Aslan, a Lion whose potency is afforded by his ability to render his observer fearful of his majesty, Beauty, or imagination, is admired by my students for its improbable availability, deemed an accessory by administrators, and thus sheepishly and flatly rejected by both respectively as something saved for students more wealthy or more worthy.

> But as for Aslan himself, the Beavers and the children didn't know what to do or say when they saw him. People who have not been in Narnia sometimes think that a thing cannot be good and terrible at the same time. If the children had ever thought so, they were cured of it now. For when they tried to look at Aslan's face they just caught a glimpse of the golden mane and the great, royal, solemn, overwhelming eyes; and then they found they couldn't look at him and went all trembly. . . . (2004, *The Narnia Chronicles*, p. 162)

What is overlooked in the beautiful halls of elite classrooms (the good) is the filth of proprietary mediocrity (the terrible). In fact, it is more likely that mediocrity lives in institutions that recruit top-dollar students from top-dollar families.

Equally, it lives in top-dollar cities. The measly charity cases who pad softly down the halls of Harvard are aspirational savants but also cautionary tales. Look here, folks, how America has failed the inner city. But yet, these clever young servants can reject the classroom because they can reject the City, thanks to Ugliness parading around as Beauty, money stuffed into her condominiums and Georgian dormitories, raining confetti from the rafters of her downtown stadiums, always making new refuse along the shoulders of her tollways.

It's really quite simple. Beauty, like Silence, evades all of us in the world where we cannot fathom being disconnected. Yet we yearn for it. And they, the students who find poetry in the interstices, in their traveling between classrooms, parking lots, and responsibilities, they build each day a way back into our own unspent Beauty; that zest to chase down a dream and get a certificate which proves the City is still worth the drive to Walmart. They entreat me to open before them a pathway to their imaginations. If only you will give us things to do so we may prove ourselves, their souls request.

And I want to tell them: stay here in these poor halls for as long as you can. Avoid the thresholds that will rip the buds from you stem to sternum. Stay here in the ugly gray classroom where the internet does not always work, where only half of the fluorescent bulbs flicker to ON any given day, and where you will not "blossom." Stay here because the City needs your Beauty, especially where angst reverberates off of the silos of academia; where what you earn determines what book we use; where what book we use determines what you learn; and what you learn determines your earning potential. Down here in the muck: this is where Beauty really spreads herself out and makes a home. She gives herself away every day here. She does not hide in the tower and make you beg for her top prize.

All of them; all of my students, they are beaming with her eager motives; fatigued but never self-righteous. They are absolutely covered in Her.

"Let the soul fall in with the ugly," said Plotinus, "and at once it shrinks within itself, denies the thing, turns away from it, out of tune, resenting it" (qtd. in Hillman, 2006, p. 215).

I want to be where Beauty does not take hold because it cannot, because it is too expensive to purchase or too expansive to understand. I want to reject its gorgeous flashing face. I long to touch back down and be filled with the failed language of Ugliness that is smeared across the City's abandoned warehouses and curled down its crumbling alleyways; in the catacombs of cubicles and corridors of drive-thru lanes; elusive Scripture of an inverted knowing.

The Soul of the City, like the Teacher, can only receive from that City what the Soul can find in that City's hideous mediocrity: the unfinished streets and boarded-up buildings screaming their poetry, the exhausted students walking without keys in their hands delivering their strife in succulent sacrifice to rows of desks each morning. They are the cost and the loss that has come backward to us from the vestiges of a culture we spent generations disordering and turning away.

So long as education in beauty and awareness of ugliness
     is considered accessory to making a living,
that is, accessory to making a life,
     music appreciation, rhetoric and elocution, poetry and
drama, studio hours that open the eye and instruct the hand
     will also be elective, accessory,
not core to the curriculum because not core to the culture.

                – James Hillman

REFERENCES

References

Abrams, D. (1996). *The spell of the sensuous: Perception and language in a more-than-human world*. New York: Random House.

Abrams, M. H., et al. (Ed.). (1975). *The Norton anthology of English literature* (Rev. ed.). New York: W.W. Norton.

Arbery, G. (2001). *Why literature matters: Permanence and the politics of reputation*. Wilmington, DE: ISI Books.

Auden, W. H. (1939, 1976). "In memory of Sigmund Freud." In F. Mendelson (Ed.), *Collected poems*. New York: Random House.

Bachelard, G. (1971). *The poetics of reverie: Childhood, language, and the cosmos*. (D. Russell, Trans.). Boston: Beacon Press.

Bachelard, G. (1994). *The poetics of space*. (M. Jolas, Trans.). Boston: Beacon Press.

Barthes, R. (1991). *The responsibility of forms: Critical essays on music, art, and representation*. (R. Howard, Trans.). Berkeley: University of California Press.

Blake, W. (1794). "Introduction to the songs of experience." Retrieved March 22, 2015, from http://www.poetryfoundation.org/.

Casey, E. (2014). "James Hillman: Philosophical intimations." In J. L. Selig & C. F. Ghorayeb (Eds.), *A tribute to James Hillman: Reflections on a renegade psychologist*. Carpinteria, CA: Mandorla Books.

Cousineau, P. (2001). "The myth of the city: From the walls of Jerusalem to the cafes of Paris." In *Once and future myths: The power of ancient stories in modern times*. Boston: Conari Press.

Cowan, D. (1988). *Unbinding Prometheus: Education for the coming age*. Dallas: Dallas Institute Publications, Dallas Institute of Humanities and Culture.

Cowan, L. (1971). *The Southern critics; an introduction to the criticism of John Crowe Ransom, Allen Tate, Donald Davidson, Robert Penn Warren, Cleanth Brooks, and Andrew Lytle*. Irving, TX: University of Dallas Press.

Deleuze, G. (1997). *Expressionism in philosophy: Spinoza*. (M. Joughin, Trans.). New York: Zone Books.

Denby, D. (2014, July 28). "Under the spell." [Review of the motion picture *Magic by moonlight*, 2014, by Woody Allen]. *The New Yorker*.

Durrell, L. (2004). "Landscape and character." In C. Willis (Ed.), *The Lawrence Durrell travel reader*. New York: Carroll & Graf.

Faulkner, W. (1992). *The Reivers: A reminiscence*. New York: Vintage.

Frank. M. (1992). *Stil in der philosophie*. Stuttgart: Reclam.

Fromm, E. (1976). *To have or to be*. New York: Harper & Row.

Gilmore, J. D. "Dallas." *On the Odessa tapes*, 2012, by the Flatlanders [CD]. New West Records.

Giroux, H. (2014). *The violence of organized forgetting: Thinking beyond America's disimagination machine.* San Francisco: City Light Books.

Gooch, B. (1993). *City poet: The life and times of Frank O'Hara.* New York: Knopf.

Gopnick, A. (2006). Foreword. *In Pictures of nothing: Abstract art since Pollock.* Princeton: Princeton University Press.

Heathcote, E. (2015, May 26). "Eccentricity is the vital ingredient for a city's success." *Financial Times.* Retrieved June 15, 2015, from http://www.ft.com/intl/cms-/s/0/adb20472-d879-11e4-ba53-00144feab7de.html#axzz3gfze2xqv.

Hedges, C., & Sacco, J. (2012). *Days of destruction, days of revolt.* New York: Nation Books.

Hillman, J. (1967). *Insearch: Psychology and religion.* Putnam, CT: Spring Publications.

Hillman, J. (1975). *Re-visioning psychology.* New York: Harper & Row.

Hillman, J. (1996). *The soul's code: In search of character and calling.* New York: Random House.

Hillman, J. (1998). *The myth of analysis: Three essays in archetypal psychology.* Evanston: Northwestern University Press.

Hillman, J. (2004). *Archetypal psychology* (Uniform ed., vol. 1). Putnam, CT: Spring Publications.

Hillman, J. (2006). *City & soul* (Uniform ed., vol. 2). (R. Leaver, Ed.). Putnam, CT: Spring Publications.

Hillman, J. (2007). *Pan and the nightmare.* Putnam, CT: Spring Publications.

Hillman, J. (2008). *Aphrodite's justice/La giustizia di Afrodite.* Naples, Italy: Edizioni La Conchiglia.

Hopkins, G. M. (1877). "God's grandeur." Retrieved February 14, 2015, from http://www.poetryfoundation.org/.

Jameson, F. (2003, May-June). "Future city," *The New Left Review*, 21. Retrieved August 8, 2013, from http://newleftreview.org/II/21/fredric-jameson-future-city.

Joyce, J. (1986). *Ulysses* (Vintage ed.). (H. Gabler, Ed.). New York: Random House.

Jung, C. G. (1984). *Civilization in transition.* In G. Adler & R.C.F. Hull (Eds. & Trans.), *Collected works of C. G. Jung* (Vol. 10). Princeton: Bollingen Series, Princeton University Press.

Kasser, T., Cohn, S., Kanner, A. D., & Ryan, R. M. (2007). "Some costs of American corporate capitalism: A psychological analysis of value and goal conflicts." *Psychological Inquiry*, 18 (1), 1-22.

Langer, S. K. (1967). *Mind, an essay on human feeling* (vol. 1). Baltimore: The Johns Hopkins University Press.

Leaver, R. (Convener) (2004, June). Talk. *Providence & beyond: An inquiry into the future of the city and the region.* Conducted from Providence, Rhode Island.

Leaver, R. (Ed.) (2006). *City & soul* (Uniform ed., vol. 2). Putnam, CT: Spring Publications.

Leslie, C. R. (Ed.) (1845). *Memoirs of the life of John Constable, esq., R.A.,* composed chiefly of his letters. London: Longman, Brown, Green and Longmans.

Levinas, E. (1999). *Otherwise than being, or beyond essence.* (A. Lingis, Trans.). Pittsburgh: Duquesne University Press.

Lewis, C. S. (2004). *The chronicles of Narnia*. New York: HarperCollins.

McLuhan, M. (2011, June 13). "Ancient quarrel in modern America." Retrieved February 15, 2015, from http://www.mcluhanonmaui.com/2011/06/ancient-quarrel-in-modern-america.html.

Miller, H. (1945). *The air-conditioned nightmare*. New York: New Directions.

Moore, T. (1994). *Soul mates: Honoring the mysteries of love and relationship*. New York: HarperPerennial.

Morton, T. (2013). Hyperobjects: *Philosophy and ecology after the end of the world*. Minneapolis: University of Minnesota Press.

Murray, G. (1927). *The classical tradition in poetry*. Cambridge, MA: Harvard University Press.

Nietzsche, F. (1999). *Kritische studienausgabe in 15 bänden* [KSA]. (G. Colli and M. Montinari, Eds.). München: Deutscher Taschenbuch Verlag.

Nixon, R. (2011). *Slow violence and the environmentalism of the poor*. Cambridge, MA: Harvard University Press.

O' Hara, F. (2008). "In Memory of my feelings" & "Meditations in an emergency." In M. Ford (Ed.), Selected poems. New York: Alfred A. Knopf.

Pavel, M. P. & Anthony, C. (2009). *Breakthrough communities: Sustainability and justice in the next American metropolis.* Cambridge, MA: MIT Press.

Paz, O. (2014). "La democracia imperial." In *Itinerario crítico, Antología de textos políticos.* Mexico City: Senado de la República/Conaculta.

Rilke, R., & Herter, M. (1910, 1964). *The notebooks of Malte Laurids Brigge*. New York: Norton.

Romanyshyn, R. (1989, 2002). *Technology as symptom and dream*. London: Routledge.

Romanyshyn, R. (2002). "Psychology is useless: Or, it should be." *In Ways of the heart: Essays toward an imaginal psychology*. Pittsburgh, PA: Trivium Publications.

Romanyshyn, R. (2014). *Leaning toward the poet: Eavesdropping on the poetry of everyday life*. Bloomington, IN: iUniverse.

Sardello, R. (1994). "City & house." In *Facing the world with soul: The reimagination of modern life.* New York: HarperPerennial.

Slattery, D. (2008). "Toward an aesthetic psychology." [Review of *City & soul* by James Hillman]. *Spring Journal*, 2 (1), 49-56.

Stevens, W. (1990). "Angel surrounded by Paysans." In *The collected poems of Wallace Stevens*. New York: Vintage Books.

Strand, M. (1998). "The night, the porch." In *Blizzard of one: Poems*. New York: Alfred A. Knopf.

Vallega, A. (2014). *Latin America philosophy from identity to radical exteriority*. Bloomington: University of Indiana Press.

Varnedoe, K. (2003, 4 May). *Pictures of nothing: Abstract art since Pollock* [audio podcast]. Retrieved from www.nga.gov/content/ngaweb/audio-video/mellon.html.

Varnedoe, K. (2006). *Pictures of nothing: Abstract art since Pollock.* Princeton: Princeton University Press.

Welty, E. (1980). "A worn path." In *The collected stories of Eudora Welty*. New York: Harcourt Brace Jovanovich.

Wittgenstein, L. (1967). *Zettel*. (G. E. M. Anscombe & G. H. von Wright, Eds.). Berkeley: University of California Press.

Wittgenstein, L. (1980). *Culture and value*. (P. Winch, Trans.). Chicago: University of Chicago Press.

Wittgenstein, L. (1981). *Tractatus logico-philosophicus*. (C. K. Ogden, Trans.). London: Routledge, Kegan & Paul.

Wittgenstein, L. (1993). *Philosophical occasions*. (J. Klagge & A. Nordmann, Eds.). Indianapolis and Cambridge: Hackett Publishing.

Wittgenstein, L. (2009). *Philosophical investigations*. (G. E. M. Anscombe, Trans.). Oxford: Wiley-Blackwell.

James Hillman Symposium 2015
Senex and Puer

Inaugurated and supported by friends of James Hillman and by scholars of his founding work in archetypal psychology, the James Hillman Symposium is the leading forum for an ongoing discussion of the *Uniform Edition*, a 10-volume collection of his writings, co-published by the Dallas Institute and Spring Publications. The mission of the conference is to encourage conversations about Hillman's major ideas and concepts in conjunction with psychological and cultural topics as well as pay tribute to his life and career.

Each of the James Hillman Symposiums takes for its subject a volume of the *Uniform Edition of the Writings of James Hillman*. The symposiums encourage participants to deepen their understanding of Hillman's writings by listening to talks given by leading scholars in diverse fields of psychology, art, theater, literature, and film—united by an appreciation of James Hillman's innovations—and by contributing to lively, stimulating discussions.

The October 2015 James Hillman Symposium will address Hillman's third volume, ***Senex and Puer.*** Senex and Puer are Latin terms for "old man" and "youth" and personify oppositional states such as old versus new, authority versus creativity, and control versus impulse. Conference themes will address these primary patterns for how we perceive ourselves and others, including time-honored myths such as the Kairos, the Great Mother, Odysseus, and Icarus to name a few.

Join us to explore this brilliant work and to celebrate the life and ideas of James Hillman. Once again the conference will take place at the Dallas Institute of Humanities and Culture, located in lively Uptown, Dallas, Texas. ***Senex and Puer*** is available for purchase from the Dallas Institute's online bookstore as well as from Spring Publications.

For more information, please visit www.dallasinstitute.org.

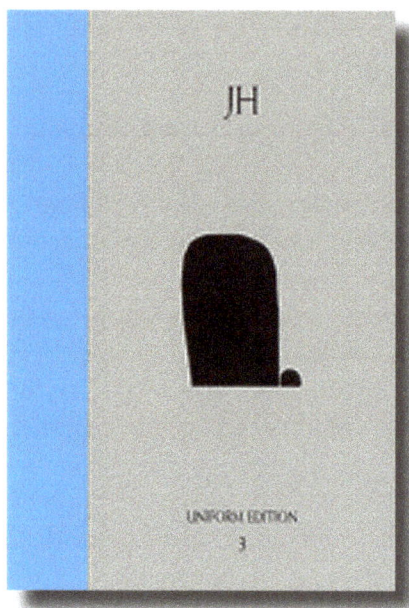

Senex and Puer

Uniform Edition Vol. 3   by JAMES HILLMAN

Edited and Introduction by Glen Slater

ISBN-13: 978-0-88214-581-5   first edition, hardcover 360 pages

Glen Slater writes in his introduction: "This volume, for the first time, collects James Hillman's running encounters with a primary psychological pattern, an archetype that arises alongside the very attempt to fashion psychological perspective."

Senex and puer are Latin terms for "old man" and "youth," and personify the poles of tradition, stasis, structure, and authority on one side, and immediacy, wandering, invention, and idealism on the other. The senex consolidates, grounds, and disciplines; the puer flashes with insight and thrives on fantasy and creativity. These diverging, conflicting tendencies are ultimately interdependent, forming two faces of the one configuration, each face never far from the other. "Old" and "new" maybe the most direct terms for the pair.

Spring Publications, in conjunction with The Dallas Institute of Humanities and Culture, publishes the *Uniform Edition of the Writings of James Hillman*, the founder of ARCHETYPAL PSYCHOLOGY—the lasting legacy of an original mind.

Uniform Edition Of The Writings Of James Hillman

The uniform, clothbound set of 10 volumes of the writings of James Hillman (also available as ebooks) unites major lectures, occasional writings, scholarly essays, clinical papers and interviews — arranged thematically. Each volume is embossed with a drawing by the American artist James Lee Byars.

ARCHETYPAL PSYCHOLOGY
Uniform Edition Vol. 1

CITY & SOUL
Uniform Edition Vol. 2

SENEX & PUER
Uniform Edition Vol. 3

FROM TYPES TO IMAGES
Uniform Edition Vol. 4

ALCHEMICAL PSYCHOLOGY
Uniform Edition Vol. 5

MYTHIC FIGURES
Uniform Edition Vol. 6

INHUMAN RELATIONS
Uniform Edition Vol. 7   (Available in 2017)

PHILOSOPHICAL INTIMATIONS
Uniform Edition Vol. 8   (Available in late 2015)

ANIMAL PRESENCES
Uniform Edition Vol. 9

CONVERSATIONS AND COLLABORATIONS
Uniform Edition Vol. 10   (Available in 2018)

To order a book - www.springpublications.com and dallasinstitute.org/publications.

References

What Is the Dallas Institute?

For over thirty years, the Dallas Institute has conducted original programs that enrich and strengthen the cultural heart of our great city. Our house on Routh Street is home for those who enjoy reading, thinking, exploring, and discussing timeless ideas that make us most fully human. The Institute has been described by our members as a "sanctuary," as an "oasis," as a "place for reflection," as "food for the soul."

Our members are the lifeblood of the Institute. It is for them that we create classes, groups, programs, and events that bring the wisdom and imagination of the humanities into their lives. If you are already a member, we thank you. If you aren't, please think about becoming a member, and join us on a common journey toward the discovery of truth, beauty, and all else that is good and noble.

The Institute's purpose is to enrich and deepen lives through the wisdom and imagination of the humanities. The humanities, as we treat them, are the written things and the spoken stories that help us define ourselves as human beings – literature, history, philosophy, politics, psychology, and mythology, among other fields.

Since 1980, the Dallas Institute has conducted public programs aimed at discovering what the humanities have to offer to the cultural life of the city, and we accomplish this through classes and group studies; through public and professional seminars; through conferences and civic involvement; through programs for school teachers and principals; and through publications.

Mission

The Dallas Institute of Humanities and Culture is a nonprofit educational organization whose purpose is to enrich and deepen the practical life of the city with the wisdom and imagination of the humanities.

Vision

The Dallas Institute of Humanities and Culture, a beacon for imaginative thought, dialogue, and programs grounded in the wisdom of the humanities, is helping to shape in positive ways our quality of life today—our conduct, traditions, decision-making, problem-solving, and creativity.

Find out more about the Dallas Institute » http://dallasinstitute.org

The Dallas Institute of Humanities and Culture

2719 Routh Street, Dallas ,Texas 75201   214- 871-2440

INDEX

Index

A

abstract art, 143, 144, 145, 158, 159
activism, 81, 85
Adler, 69, 158
aesthetics, 4, 5, 25, 33, 79, 81, 82, 83, 84, 85, 87, 88, 93, 94, 95–97, 129
aesthetics of place, 33
alchemy, 38, 80
analysis, 50, 60, 69, 74, 75, 124, 143, 158
animal, 15, 17, 35, 53, 68, 94, 111, 114, 117
anima mundi, 37, 59, 123, 126, 149
anxiety, 52, 69, 73
Aphrodite, 67, 74, 95, 96, 124, 132, 158
appetite, 106, 107, 124
archetypal imagination, 21, 23, 25, 27, 29, 135
archetypal psychology, 24, 37, 38, 39, 40, 47, 58, 59, 60, 76, 78, 86, 116–18, 128, 132, 135, 158, 161, 162
artist, 16, 17, 48, 55, 68, 86, 90, 137, 144, 162
Auden, W. H., 3, 37, 133, 157
awareness, 4, 5, 15, 79, 88, 95, 98–102, 123, 126, 129, 135, 150, 154

B

Bachelard, Gaston, 2, 15, 107, 122, 126, 157
baroque, 119, 120
bench, 3, 21, 37, 38, 39, 40, 41, 43–45, 47, 51, 106
betrayal, 59, 62, 131, 132
body politic, 3, 57, 59–65
Borges, 17
brain, 15–16, 124, 130, 149
Brazil, 4, 116, 118–19
breath, 2, 38, 84, 93
bridge, 2, 24, 25–26, 59, 62, 135
building, 3, 35, 50, 53, 63, 81, 131, 147

C

H

I

J

N

O

P

U

V

W

Y

Z

www.ingramcontent.com/pod-product-compliance
Lightning Source LLC
Chambersburg PA
CBHW061222270326
41927CB00022B/3471